The Journey Inward

FOUR SEASONS OF REFLECTION
FOR DEEP HEALING AND TRANSFORMATION

TIFFANY TYLER-GARNER, PHD

ISBN: 978-1-966798-30-9

I dedicate this book to my village.

Table of Contents

Starting a New Season!

In 2024, I began the year with an exhaustion that could only be overcome by finally doing the work—the work of finding myself, boundaries, and peace. After years of running from poverty, struggling with perfectionism, and drowning in self-doubt, I finally acknowledged that I was a chronic people pleaser who had become resentful beyond joy.

I was unhappy with myself, the people in my life, the state of the world, and seemingly my inability to change anything. It was the new year, but I didn't have any new resolve. After attending a special women's group on processing and purpose, I decided I was done with making New Year's resolutions. Instead, I committed to a year of reflection. What resulted was a powerful year of healing and the birth of a new season!

Now, I'm grabbing a pen and helping others begin a new season. No longer bound by fear of failure or success, but cognizant of the ways in which our conscious and unconscious beliefs drive our success or demise, I chronicled my year of transformation in hopes of empowering others to find their voice, set boundaries, and transform the conditions that have them bound.

As an educational psychologist, published researcher, and proven servant leader, I have been recognized as "Humanitarian of the Year," "Alumna of the Year," and a "Workforce Development Champion." I have served as a member of a governor's cabinet, a CEO, a COO, and an executive director. Moreover, my personal journey is a story of triumph.

I survived molestation, sexual assault, dropout, and divorce to become degreed, remarried, and a recognized leader in my community. However, my greatest success is finally overcoming me—overcoming how I saw myself, loved myself, and loved others.

The Journey Inward: Four Seasons of Reflection for Deep Healing and Transformation chronicles my yearlong journey of deep healing through the practice of reflection. What began as a series of reflections shared on Facebook has become an unearthing! The birth of a new season founded on transparency, centered in authenticity, and grounded in healing.

Readers are supported to unpack, uncouple, and understand the ways their thoughts, practices, and results are informed by their unconscious and conscious beliefs. Likened to seasons, over the course of this year long journey, readers are shown the transparent musings of a leader grappling with imposter syndrome, transgenerational trauma, toxicity, and codependence in hopes of empowering readers to take charge of their life by finding their voice, setting intention, and letting go of status quo living.

Attention is given to leveraging the authentic self, family narrative, and boundaries as sustainable strategies for finding purpose, managing conflict, and sustaining personal growth. Complex topics are explored through my lived experience as a woman committed to embracing a new season in my leadership, love life, parenting, relationships, and identity. I explore a range of topics and timely issues, including:

- Perfectionism
- Mean Girl Culture
- Imposter Syndrome
- Acculturation
- Trauma and Abuse
- Exceptionalism
- Resilience
- Loss
- Forgiveness
- Attachment

- Relationships
- Parenting
- Setting Boundaries

Through this journey, I share invaluable insights about leadership, resilience, healing, and change. Readers are empowered to transform themselves and their conditions. A new season begins through—the journey inward!

Join me on this journey toward healing, hope, and a new season!

The Journey Inward as a Framework for Healing and Transformation

The Journey Inward: Four Seasons of Reflection for Deep Healing and Transformation reflects the four seasons of my transformative yearlong journey. It begins with a winter characterized by despondency, a breaking point, and a new beginning—the beginning of my healing. The winter season is followed by my spring, a spring of exploration, possibilities, and a new resolve. My spring season is followed by a summer of radical truth, fierce boundary setting, and a resolute commitment to having the life I want, while fighting toxicity. I conclude by sharing the musing of my fall season, a season of clarity and a search for guiding universal principles. Accordingly, you will note the journey is organized into four seasons: winter, spring, summer, and fall.

Each season or section begins by highlighting key lessons from each season, followed by a series of reflections. Each reflection concludes with what I call "the work," several key questions to consider from the theme of the reflection.

I encourage readers to ponder the key themes and questions in hopes of unearthing the conscious and unconscious beliefs driving their choices each day. Attention is given to modeling the power of reflection and exploring the issues impacting our daily lives. Readers are also offered some practical strategies along the way.

As you embark on this journey, consider beginning the practice of daily reflection. Push yourself to go beyond venting to unpacking. Unpack the challenges of the day, long-standing issues, and the areas or principles foundational to your identity, mindset, practices, and principles. Be sure to prioritize key areas of your experience, including:

- family history
- your identity

- relationships with family, friends, and colleagues
- your problem-solving approach
- your conflict resolution style
- your core values and guiding principles
- each of the major domains of your life, such as career, health, finances, and spirituality
- pervasive or persistent stressors, challenges, or obstacles
- opportunities; especially missed, realized, or stalled opportunities

As you reflect on each of these areas, challenge yourself to give words to how you are feeling, thinking, hearing, and seeing the issue or opportunity at hand. In the case of my journey, these musings manifested as the reflections that followed.

Whether written as a poem, indictment, call to action, or a fleeting thought, note what you are experiencing. Follow by asking yourself, *What might I consider further?*

This consideration is "The Work."

I title it "The Work" because it is the exercise of unpacking what has surfaced for you. It is designed to help you go beyond complaining, compartmentalizing, externalizing and projecting to helping you make the vital connection to the season that is being ushered in. It is a catalyst for identifying:

- the lesson
- the opportunity
- the approach
- the principle
- the practice
- the strategy

It is where you turn the corner, find a new horizon, or come to a resolution.

Accordingly, read the key lessons for the season and each reflection. Then ask yourself the questions identified in the work section. Once you have answered the questions in "The Work" section, identify one lesson, opportunity, strategy, principle, approach, or practice that you will adopt to address the theme.

You may also identify your own questions or work to consider. "The Work" noted in this book reflects my areas of transformation. However, you may find that the reflections result in different questions for you. Go with it!

Identify and respond to the work that surfaces for you! Also, be sure to adopt whatever resulting change manifests. Note this change as a commitment that you will make to yourself or others.

To support your growth, each reflection and season concludes with the question, "With these new insights or awareness, what commitment will I make to myself or others?"

Complete this prompt by indicating at least one commitment you will make to yourself or others. This commitment could be a change in approach, practice, or mindset. The commitment could be the next step you will take to ensure progress or your success. This commitment can be a declaration like "I will consistently communicate for clarity." The commitment can also be a commitment that you make to others. For example, you may commit to calling a parent each week or meeting with your team at work biweekly.

I encourage you to lean into your healing and transformation. Identify an action or change you can make to foster your healing and transformation. This is your journey, as supported by my journey to deep healing and transformation through reflection.

Now, let's begin!

Winter

I began the year with an exhaustion that could only be overcome by doing the work. For years, I had stuffed down, bottled, and compartmentalized every hurt in pursuit of success. In 2020, I would find myself on the sidelines of my own life.

If one's journey could be likened to seven years of plenty and seven years of famine, the pandemic would become the signaling of a dread to come. I would go from being the first doctor and CEO in my family to a public failure that was all-consuming. It had consumed my confidence, my reputation, and any hope I had for achieving the aspirations that had once been my guide. In its wake, fear, shame, and doubts that would take years to overcome were left.

Fearful that another year of unrealized resolutions would only confirm my fears, in 2024, I made a bold commitment to finally doing the work—the work of healing, discovery, and peace. I made a yearlong commitment to processing what was happening to me.

From this journey, I have discovered so many truths and opportunities. Like turning on a windshield wiper, my vision is clearing. It all began with a chance encounter in a hardware store.

While in a hardware store, I happened upon a fellow leader in the community. I had previously made her acquaintance, but I didn't know much about her beyond her dedication to youth in the foster care system. I faintly recollected that she had overcome several life challenges, but I didn't know much about her personal journey. I was also certain that she didn't know mine.

Truthfully, I had spent so much time running away from my story and trying to be what I thought successful people were, I doubted anyone really knew me. Moreover, over the course of my journey, I discovered that I didn't know myself. In our chance encounter, she invited me to a gathering of local women where the focus was processing and finding purpose. This chance encounter would be the beginning of a new season.

As my journey unfolded, I discovered it could be likened to seasons. My first season was a winter characterized by despondency, a breaking point, and a new beginning–the beginning of my healing. It was different from any period that preceded it. It was a complex interplay of discovery, ongoing challenge, and new insight. I had begun a new job and returned to work at a governmental entity at the behest of the department director. My husband had returned to school. Both of my children were living on their own. I had determined that I could no longer manage trying to be what everyone else needed. I was losing myself, losing pace, and losing peace in ways that felt unsurmountable.

I was also discovering some truths and facing some hard lessons. During this season, a key lesson was the importance of checking the narratives by which I live and see the world.

Check the Narrative

One of the greatest gifts I received during my winter season was the gift of my grandfather's story. Nearly 6 months before his passing, at the age of 96 years old, he shared the story of his diaspora. While not a diaspora in the traditional sense because Louisiana was never our ancestral home, it was the story of his leaving.

What was most powerful was that it was HIS story. It was not the narrative that had been told for years, the story of a young father who left six children and my grandmother while absconding with her savings. It was not his children's story, the story of a man who left an emotional hole in their souls, and in his wake gave rise to fear, low esteem, and a longing that could not be soothed. It was his retelling.

Slowly, he recounted how he, his brother, and cousin fled Tallulah, Louisiana, in the middle of the night. As if reliving the time, he shared how they worked from sunup to sundown in the fields for 50 cents a day. He noted how they were prohibited from owning a home or property.

His telling was the unraveling of the desolate fabric in which we had wrapped our expectations for men, fathers, and marriage. In some respects, I had been freed from the beliefs that men:

- don't stay
- don't care
- aren't safe as partners

At the altar of my grief and abandonment, I had been given a golden opportunity to unpack the fears that belie spoken and unspoken rules like a woman should always have:

- some "mad money"
- her own account
- no expectations for what a man will or will not do

In the gift of his story were the pearls of his resilience, the humanization of men, and the hope of loving differently.

With my yearlong commitment to reflection underway, I decided to unpack the gift of his story this season. In the process, I unearthed some powerful new narratives and a healing that has transcended generational hurts and birthed a new legacy.

One of the first things to result from my unpacking was an expansion of "the record." Until now, I had not realized how I had been given a record and was keeping score. This record was not only an accounting but an album that played over and over again.

I was given a record akin to a patchwork quilt, bits and pieces of everyone else's experience of my grandfather's absence. Troublingly, this "quilt" was held together by skewed things, unspoken things, tears, and compounding hurts, all weaved together through the eyes of children too young to understand the complexities of relationships and too hurt to move beyond the emotional age of his leaving.

If you have not done so, it is vital that you go back and unpack your hurts. It is critical to get to a resolution. You may discover the story is:

- not the whole story.
- not the real story.
- not your story at all!

After much reflection and consideration, I realized that the hurts that informed my narrative were not always my hurts. In some instances, I was dutifully carrying generational trauma. In other instances, I didn't have the story at all. I had the story the children were told or the retelling of adult whispers.

When it was all said and done, I realized our family story also could be told as:

- My grandfather fled the rural, segregated south and a life of sharecropping in hopes of a better life with other men from his family.
- My grandfather would go on to become a homeowner, a husband of 40+ years, and a man with an unwavering work ethic.
- Fearing for my grandfather's safety, my grandmother told her employer that she didn't want anything from her children's

father and that he fled the town with another woman when her employer said, "We will make him come back and take care of his responsibilities!"

With the addition of his story, my "record" was transformed. I began accounting for things like my grandmother and my grandfather's sister being best friends throughout their lives. I realized that my aunts and mother were sent to Los Angeles, where their paternal family resided. I began to see my marriage as an opportunity to be loved. I shifted how I saw my sons, the inevitably of them becoming husbands and fathers, and the fact that they were men. I checked our narrative, and my story changed.

As my journey unfolded, it was like a muddying of the waters. The more I reflected on the issues I faced and explored the themes I was confronting, I realized my experience was heavily informed by stories I had been told, other people's truths, generational trauma and pathology, and a patchwork of hurts. There were the stories I heard about why my grandfather left, how my grandmother hurt others, and how two generations of children felt largely abandoned. Not until my mother heard my grandfather's retelling of his diaspora did I question the hurts I accepted as truth.

For years, I believed men leave, women stay begrudgingly, and children bear the weight of never being good enough for their parents to be happy. As I unpacked all I had been told, I realized much of what I believed, lived down to or up to, or perpetuated could not be understood without first realizing the dangers of family enmeshment. My story and the life I was unconsciously living were enmeshed in generations of hurt. However, my future did not have to be entangled in anything but my choices.

The gift of this season was realizing I had a choice, and, with it the ability to choose to lay down other people's grievances, hurts, lenses, perspectives, and anything else that would stand in the way of me knowing myself and choosing happiness. This muddying of the waters was a reframing. I had muddied how my family talked about relationships, our past, and our ability to manifest change. I had muddied what we said and believed. This muddying of things was transformative. It became the soil I needed to grow something different than what my family had reaped for generations.

If you have ever found yourself fighting other people's battles, holding other people's grudges, or unhappy because everyone around you is constantly unhappy, I encourage you to:

- Forgive yourself and forgive others for being all you could be, or they could be as people leading an unexamined life. You did not have the awareness, capacity, or bandwidth to wield "choice" in the ways that one can when you discover you have options.
- Acknowledge that you may not have had a great set of options at a particular crossroad in your life, but you can work to create them. As you uncouple your decisions from family trauma, your past, and other people's agenda or needs, you will discover that you have the option of saying no, changing your mind, leaving, staying, growing, or whatever YOUR needs dictate. Your emotional needs, physical needs, desires, and expectations can become a healthy compass when you uncouple your decision-making from pleasing people, codependency, and other counterproductive behavior.
- Get clear about what you believe and why you believe it. Be sure that your beliefs are rooted in reality and free from the residue of other people's pain. For years, I believed I was not enough because I was born in shame, prey to stereotypes and gender

bias, and operating from the faulty belief that I must perform myself into worth. Imagine how empowering it has been to discover that by virtue of who I am, I'm redefining what it is to be a woman, Black, a leader, a wife, and a mother. Before, I strove to be each of these things, as if I could fail at them. I now know I am each of these things, and my choices define what they are for me. I am a woman, and I have decided that means that I can embrace the full range of my femininity without living down to the diatribe of being angry or strong. I am Black, and my blackness does not require a reference or an attestation. I am articulate, smart, professional, and diplomatic, and I do not act like any other race when I demonstrate these inherent dimensions of my personality or blackness. I am a leader, mother, and wife. These roles are not synonymous with being unyielding, saving, or failing. I can inhabit each of these roles with the grace, confidence, and the interdependence needed because I am not required to be wrong, right, or an imposter. I am only requiring self-acceptance now. I no longer require myself to be whatever others need.

As you read the reflections that follow, I hope you will muddy the waters too. Don't passively accept any definition or standard that does not serve or honor you.

Chapter 1: The Gift of Acceptance

One day, my husband said, "Tiffany, for everything they weren't, they were everything they could be."

It compelled me to consider what gifts we miss when we wrap our experiences of others in our expectations.

Much like unwrapping the same gift repeatedly and expecting something different, sometimes we show up to our relationships expecting them to be something they cannot be.

Today, I am grounding my relationships in acceptance. I am embracing everyone as they are and not as I hope them to be.

Imagine the ways we subtly communicate to others that they are inadequate because we keep hoping that they will eventually be who we believe we need.

What if we accepted that people are who they can be; a state that is not dictated by our needs or desires but rather one informed by their purpose and experience.

What if we are waiting on things they were never intended to give us?

It's like showing up to a strawberry patch and expecting peaches. Eventually, we must acknowledge that these perceived limitations aren't limitations. Rather, they are merely who they are.

Our needs and wants are not factors in their identity unless they choose them to be.

What if we choose to accept that they are giving us all that they can?

What if all others are ever giving us is all they can give us?

This season and every day forward, I give myself and others the gift of this acceptance.

The Work:

1. How might my relationships be transformed if I accepted others for who they are, not as I wish them to be?

2. How might my experience be transformed if I released the belief that others must be what we need?

3. What would happen if I accepted that my past was as it should be?

With these new insights or awareness, what commitment will I make to myself or others?

_____

_____

_____

_____

_____

Chapter 2: Sometimes There Is No Bad Guy

The older I get, the more I realize that sometimes there is no bad guy.

Despite my best efforts to understand why some things happen, sometimes there is no culprit. Moreover, as I come to the realization that most people are just doing the best that they can, I am realizing there is no villain.

Every calamity or tragedy of errors doesn't have an enemy. There are things that happen just because things happen.

The leak, the death, the break, the snap, the pull, and the hole don't always conspire, and sometimes, there is no conspiracy.

With this new awareness, I am compelled to pivot from hunting down the bad guy to creating the life I want.

Other people may not ever be able to help themselves, but I commit to helping me—HEAL!

With this awareness, I hope others will consider developing a new list of requirements. Declaratively I say, I will no longer require myself or others to:

- find the culprit
- place blame
- make excuses
- be sorry

Once upon a time, I thought people had to be sorry for me to heal. I also thought if I just rounded up all of the culprits, I could prevent bad things from happening.

Life has taught me that the only thing that becomes imprisoned on the quest of finding the bad guy is me. I get handcuffed to the trauma. I get locked up with the pain. I unknowingly do a life sentence with what happened.

So this season, I free myself. I free myself from the expectation of finding someone wrong. I release the need to determine who is at fault. I forgo the chance to point fingers.

I choose me!

The Work:

1. Am I falsely assuming intent when an affront occurs?

2. Is an apology requisite to my healing in this instance?

3. If no one else takes responsibility, can I be responsible for moving myself forward?

With these new insights or awareness, what commitment will I make to myself or others?

_____

_____

_____

_____

_____

Chapter 3: Forgive Yourself

May you forgive yourself for the things that never required an apology.

Release yourself from the guilt and shame of:

- learning
- trauma
- regret
- closed doors
- failed or seasonal relationships
- your victimization

There is no apology needed for:

- giving all you had
- doing what you could
- making decisions from what you knew at the time

Stop apologizing for being the only thing you could be. Allow yourself to be okay with not being more of anything.

This season, forgive yourself for not being taller, lighter, or smaller. Stop apologizing for being loving, forgiving, or passionate.

Stop conflating your worth with other people's limitations, inadequacies, and shortcomings.

This season, walk in the light of grace, growing and gaining. Celebrate the triumph of trying. Embrace the growth that results from learning. Acknowledge the gains that come through practice.

Grade yourself on a curve while you're on your learning curve. Create the psychological and emotional space you need to be your best yourself by recognizing that becoming better requires practice; it's the inevitable process of trial and error.

The Work:

1. Am I giving myself the grace needed to grow?

2. Have I accepted that the past has passed?

3. Will I allow myself the gift of being who I am?

With these new insights or awareness, what commitment will I make to myself or others?

_____

_____

_____

_____

_____

Chapter 4: Who Gives This Woman

As I contemplate what it took to remarry, I liken it to the part of the wedding ceremony where the officiant says, "Who gives this woman to be married?"

At one time, I was given by my grandmother's hurts, my mother's fear, and my father's absence. At some points, I was not given at all. They held onto me tightly, praying I was getting it right. In other instances, my ideas about marriage gave me so it was a fanciful rendition of a storybook ending that could not be sustained.

Still, other times, it was my husband saying, "Tiffany, are you hearing me or hearing your fears?"

In one instance, it was everyone I had ever dated. One by one, the failings of those relationships lined up in something akin to a litmus test. The tyranny did not end until my husband said, "I am not any of those people. I'm who I have shown you."

Still, other times, other people's expectations tried to give me. These were equally hard to follow. It was a complex mix of other people's hurts, expectations, and fears.

Finally, I decided I would give myself to be married. It was the best decision I ever made. I jumped the broom and with it:

- the reasons why my grandfather left
- the people who didn't stay
- the fairy tale
- other people's expectations of toxic narratives about men, women, and relationships

I jumped the broom, hopped right into my husband's arms, and into:

- my own decisions
- my hopes
- my dreams

If you are contemplating leaving singleness and are considering being given, I strongly encourage you to consider by whom or what.

If you are given by a need for acceptance, begin with self-acceptance. If you are given by a need for love, begin with self-love. If you are given by a need for identity, know that it is critical to be a Ms. before a Mrs. It is imperative to have a clear sense of self before joining with another.

I am also finding that it is critical to give yourself over each day to the conviction, compromise, communication, compassion, and consistency marriage requires.

This season, join me in considering who or what is giving you to your next great chapter. Take the time to heal, know yourself and understand what your expectations are and from where they come. Also, consider that marriages evolve as each partner evolves, as your life roles evolve, and as life happens. Not being clear about when you are in transition and not having a game plan for transition can be detrimental.

As I have unpacked what I've been given by, some of the most powerful insights have been:

- the reasons why I chose relationships
- what I believed happened in relationships
- the ways fear, belonging, early attachment, and generational pathology can drive relationship decisions.

I have chosen relationships for many reasons, including other people's expectations, societal expectations, and an unwillingness to make a hard decision. None of these reasons are sufficient for sustaining relationships.

Once I chose and stayed because I wanted to ensure my children had their father. Unfortunately, this reason did not help us account for the other things that happen in marriages. In another instance, I chose it for religious reasons. Unfortunately, not having the willpower to sustain celibacy but having the conviction to resist fornication was not a blueprint for sustaining marriage. By the time I chose marriage again and was successfully navigating it and its evolution and transitions, several things had happened:

- I was financially independent, so I was no longer driven by fear of poverty. As a result, we have been able to place our strategies for managing finances, inflation, and recessionary impacts in a more objective context. Changes in the economy no longer feel like a life-and-death situation.
- I had completed four college degrees, which gave me a lot of practice and a framework for considering other people's perspectives, feelings, and the ways in which systemic issues impinge upon the individual experience and relationships. The mindset of a learner has supported me to ask different questions when we experience challenges. Before, I would say, "What are you doing wrong?" or "What are you doing to us?" Now, I am practiced enough to ask, "What might account for what we are experiencing, thinking, and feeling?"
- My children are independent adults who have an active independent relationship with their biological father. As a result, my decision to marry was not solely predicated on giving them a father. I weighed my individual needs, interests, and passions in new ways. I considered things like our shared faith,

our convictions, our shared sense of humor, and the fact that we could talk and sit in silence, and it was comforting. Most importantly, I weighed that I could be emotionally naked and loved. These things had never been considered during other phases of my life.

I share this new awareness to suggest that knowing yourself, knowing your why, and knowing the other person well is vital. The woman who began mothering at 20 years old and married didn't know any of these things. I also hadn't accounted for our significant cultural differences. While I am thankful for our 11-year season, I am also mindful that I fumbled through our time together with the weight of generational trauma, daddy issues, and a young brain that was still developing.

If someone asks now, "Who gives this woman?" It's me! I give myself— wholly, from our shared expectations, and with a game plan for staying married! Who gives you?

The Work:

1. From where am I choosing marriage or relationships? From what perspective, need, history, or expectation?

2. From what criteria, expectations, standards, or needs am I choosing my partner?

3. What values, gifts, expectations, priorities, or needs am I bringing to the relationship?

With these new insights or awareness, what commitment will I make to myself or others?

_____

_____

_____

_____

_____

Chapter 5: Uncoupled

As I process the things that trouble me, I realize that I have coupled or tied my peace to other people's choices, moods, and aims.

I have coupled my sense of efficacy to other people's praise, affirmation, and criticism.

I have coupled my identity to other people's expectations, needs, and desires.

I have coupled my aspirations to other people's hopes, dreams, and wishes.

I have even coupled my well-being to other people's dysfunction, mental health issues, and problems.

It is time to uncouple. I can no longer allow my identity, peace, and sense of worth to be driven by things outside of me.

These things are inside work for a reason.

How I see myself, feel, and what I believe about my possibilities should never be determined by somebody else.

When I put my worth, hopes, and aspirations in other people's hands, I do something worse than leaving these things to chance, I leave them to things like:

- other people's agendas
- whims
- bias
- dysfunction

When I do not hold firm to my moral compass, emotional thermostat, and sense of self, I can be subjected to an emotional roller coaster that is exacerbated by toxic environments, codependent relationships, and dysfunction.

I cannot couple my identity to work, my ability to protect or save others, or anything outside of my identity in Christ. When I do, I leave my very existence to something worse than chance.

This season, I am uncoupling my peace, identity, and well-being. This season, I will live unbound!

The Work:

1. In what is my identity rooted? How do I identify these dimensions, characteristics, or facets? Do these definitions of self serve me?

2. Have I defined balance or homeostasis for myself? When I am balanced, what practices, thinking, or approach am I employing to maintain balance? When I am imbalanced, what factors or root causes are at play?

3. How can I internally identify and maintain priorities, expectations, goals, and standards that enable me to maintain peace, joy, self-love, and boundaries?

With these new insights or awareness, what commitment will I make to myself or others?

_____

_____

_____

_____

_____

Chapter 6: What Is Making Peace?

Yesterday, "making peace" was powerfully reframed for me.

I always thought it was accepting what happens. Yesterday, I discovered a new definition.

Making peace is not about accepting whatever happens. Rather, it is the acknowledgment that something has happened and a commitment to doing what can be done in its wake.

In so many areas of our lives, we are called to make peace with things. In my life, I have had to make peace with:

- the absence of a parent
- a divorce
- the ending of a season
- a public crisis

Daily, we are required to make peace with other people's decisions, behaviors, and actions.

Like the serenity prayer, I have had to make peace with things I cannot change.

Recently, while responding to my inner critic, imposter syndrome surfaced. I happened upon a chronic gas lighter in my life. I was already struggling with whether I was worthy of being invited to an upcoming event, and then they essentially asked, "Why are you going to be there?"

Unfortunately, I didn't pause to consider if they were really asking why they weren't invited.

At a time, when I should have been jubilant about an opportunity on the horizon, I was panicking. I feared the person would block the opportunity. I feared they would besmirch my reputation as they often did to anyone who had the courage to leave them.

Rather than being emboldened by the ways in which others were recognizing my gifts, I was reduced to the murmurings of the little girl who never fit in.

Even worse, I had allowed the bullying and gossip that frequently ensued to cause me to question if I was sure I was good enough.

As the water-cooler chatter reverberated, so did the familiar echoes of imposter syndrome.

Thankfully, there is a group of women in my life whom I lovingly reference as my midwives and sisters. I also have a loving husband and family who love me in spite of me. Unsettled, I asked each of them to pray for me.

I noted I would be participating in an activity that was compelling me to make peace with my journey in ways that had unsettled me.

Powerfully, they began reframing "making peace."

Some noted I had peace, and that was the foundation of being able to tell one's story. Another noted that I had always been able to make peace, and that ability fueled my achievements. Still, others noted peace is the ability to reconcile one's story.

As a result, I now believe making peace doesn't require me to:

- go along
- accept anything
- turn a blind eye or deaf ear
- pretend
- avoid
- hurt

Rather "making peace" is a freeing of one's self from the expectation that:

- you can change the past
- you can change people
- an apology is needed to heal
- our experiences, truths, and perspectives must match other people's experiences, truths, or perspectives

When I make peace in this way, I can leave the past. I can leave old hurts and unhealthy relationships in the past. I can forgive myself and others. I can acknowledge and release myself from old versions of me. I can release myself from things, places, and people that no longer serve me. I can move on without an apology. I can release myself from projects and people who won't take accountability for their healing or progress.

When I make peace in this new way, I can go:

- forward
- in a new direction
- without you
- with you
- through it

I can go on!

This season and every day forward, I will make peace in a new way. I will do it in ways that give me peace instead of leaving me in pieces.

The Work:

1. Are there areas in my life where I feel disquieted? If so, where and why? What is needed to find peace or resolution in these areas? How can I define peace in ways that will enable me to execute without cooperation or expectation from others?

2. How can I move beyond lamenting my past to maximizing my present and building my future? How can I demonstrate that I have uncoupled my identity and sense of worth from other people's approval?

3. How do I begin to see myself as worthy? Am I substituting external affirmation for internal confirmation? Have I decided my ability to move forward is contingent upon someone else's approval? If so, how can I shift this faulty thinking to reinforce my agency?

With these new insights or awareness, what commitment will I make to myself or others?

_____

_____

_____

_____

_____

Chapter 7: Release

In a moment of distress, I asked myself, *Where am I showing up from? Who's showing up?*

In that moment, I saw the unhealed parts of me.

I saw the little girl who wondered whether every man would stay because the first one left.

I saw the awkward teenager, the one bullied for being different, asking too many questions, and always raising her hand.

I saw the little girl who was told, "Don't tell anyone!" and the young woman who was told, "They'll never believe you!"

I saw every news channel I had ever seen while growing up. Whether it was the worst eyewitness, the one who saw everything in slang, or the countless depictions or narratives that affirmed that people like me don't make it, I saw my fears.

As I panned out, I saw the ways I ruminate about or rehearse every mistake and the ways I'm still apologizing for things I can't change, like my demographics, my earliest zip codes, or my very being.

As I looked around to see who was showing up or where I was coming from, I saw me.

I saw the woman still trying to outrun poverty, still trying to live down prejudice, and still trying to be enough.

Strangely, I could not see the girl who had lived, the young woman who had grown, and the woman who succeeded; the resilient one.

Somehow, in my moments of distress, the little girl, the survivor, was showing up; the one that didn't realize she had survived.

Somehow, in all my glory and resilience, I couldn't find a single doctor, not Dr. Tyler, not Dr. Tyler-Garner, not anyone or anything I hoped would save me.

There was no title big enough to save me or usher me into wholeness, and I had tried many:

- Doctor
- COO
- President
- Executive Director
- Humanitarian of the Year
- Alumna of the Year

Maybe this was a signal that it was time to try just being Tiffany and being okay with that.

Whatever it was, I am certain that it was time for me to release some things.

This season, I release the need to be:

- right
- liked
- perfect
- accepted
- revered

No longer will I be bound by or tied to old hurts, or all the younger versions of me, the ones uncertain about whether I will make it.

This season, I am committed to releasing the things that no longer serve me.

I'm beginning with my relationship with myself. It's time-out for being my own worst enemy and my biggest critic.

I'm relinquishing my need to punish myself through my words or deeds. I give up negative self-talk, overeating, and overthinking. If it's not loving or kind, I'm no longer saying it to myself.

I'm taking a page from the good book:

"...whatsoever things are true, whatsoever things are honest, whatsoever things are just, whatsoever things are pure, whatsoever things are lovely, whatsoever things are of good report; if there be any virtue, and if there be any praise, think on these things." Philippians 4:8

I'm changing:

- my self-talk
- my walk
- ME!

I am also revisiting:

- my priorities
- how I show up
- where and how I spend my time
- where I invest
- who has access to me
- who gets the gift of me

If I'm not on my list, I'm rewriting the list.

I'm also rewriting the script, erasing and redoing the tape, and changing the narrative.

I'm grabbing the pen! I'm writing my own story!

This season, I'm releasing anything that does not serve me, and I'm embracing myself!

The Work:

1. What beliefs, expectations, standards, or principles am I holding about me, who I should be or could become? Are they helpful or hurtful? Are they attainable? Are they untenable? Have they been exceeded? Are they empowering or disempowering? Are they really mine?

2. Am I periodically updating my beliefs, narratives, expectations, standards, and principles to reflect the current reality of my situation? Are there areas in my life where I am willfully living in the past? Am I feeling stagnant presently because I have not reconciled some inherent dissonance occurring in my life? How can I begin building a future of my making?

3. How can I align what I say, feel, and think with the future I want? If I do, what practices, processes, and partnerships are occurring? What factors or criteria will I consistently monitor to ensure I remain in alignment?

With these new insights or awareness, what commitment will I make to myself or others?

_____

_____

_____

_____

_____

Chapter 8: Whose Voice Are You Hearing?

Sometimes, I can't hear my voice. Sometimes, I wonder if I even have one. More often than not, I hear expectations, beliefs, hopes and dreams, and fears, that I am not even sure are mine.

I'm holding space for the first man that broke my grandmother's heart or the dream my mother had when she said, "And this too shall pass!"

In this moment, I am realizing there is no room for constructive criticism, only what feels like the literal deconstruction of my hopes, my dreams, and my willingness to try again.

I got to find my voice! The one that rings clear in the face of other people's misconceptions, misconstruals, and misgivings. I need a voice that tells me who I am and reminds me when people try to distract, deflect, and defy my ability to overcome!

I got to find my voice! I'm not sure where I lost it. Maybe it was the first time someone said:

- "Don't tell anyone!"
- "Who told you that you could be that, do that, see that?"
- "Who told you that you could BE?"
- "Who do you think you are?"

Wherever I lost it. Wherever it is! I must find it.

This season, I will find my voice!

The Work:

1. How can I stand up for myself when I face resistance?

2. Am I allowing others to dictate things that should be internally defined, like my goals, preferences, and desires?

3. How can I set and maintain boundaries that honor the vision I have for my life?

With these new insights or awareness, what commitment will I make to myself or others?

_____

_____

_____

_____

_____

Chapter 9: The Residue of Silence

A residue builds in the wake of prolonged silence. It's a thin film of doubt. It seizes and then gives way to fear. As I considered the support I received after sharing, I was disquieted.

I didn't want anyone to feel bad for me, including me. Even though it was bad and I felt bad, I somehow felt worse because others acknowledged my pain and cared.

I wondered, was this discomfort the result of feeling undeserving? While I haven't grown enough to consider how I am contributing to my invisibility by denying these acknowledgments, I am beginning to unpack my discomfort.

It's a paradox. I lament being invisible but cannot bear or accept others seeing me.

My identity has become so tied to the mask that when I lift it, I feel shame. Imagine expecting people to pretend with you but being mad that you have to pretend.

I know I can't have it both ways. I don't comfortably stand in my truth, but I can't hide the truth anymore.

It's as if I have emerged from a cocoon but I am not flying yet.

I am in this ugly in-between. I am more of myself but still unsure of myself. The narratives of my past make me feel unsure. In the shadows are the old messages like:

- "Who do you think you are?"
- "You just want somebody to look at you!"
- "Ain't nobody thinking about you!"

What do you do when these things are true?

I do want to be seen. I want to be heard, even while I cry.

At times, I have wanted someone else to acknowledge what happened to me and say, "I'm sorry."

I do want others to care about me and think about how they treat me.

What I do not want is for it to be shameful.

I want to be free and heal, but the acknowledgement of my trauma is not palatable. I can't swallow it. It does not go down easily. The shame of surviving threatens to choke me sometimes.

Even the complexity of this makes me ponder. *How can I be feeling dirty again? How can I be feeling dirty decades later? Can I still be dirty?*

Maybe it's like being soiled. Maybe you have to emotionally wipe yourself clean in the wake of abuse. As I consider my fear, I realize I may still be sitting in the darkness and dirt of it emotionally.

When I first told, no one had the emotional bandwidth or capacity to help me unpack it. Everyone around me was dealing with their own trauma. Generations of trauma had converged to leave me uncovered, unkempt, and unsupported.

In this moment, I now know only God has the ability to cleanse me.

Unfortunately, knowing they didn't have the capacity to help me did not stop me from seeking their support. I think I hoped that they could look past their pain and see mine. It's more likely that my pain only reminded them of their pain.

They could not see me because they could not stand to see themselves. They could not bear that it had happened again. They could not bear that it happened on top of their hurt or on their watch. But somehow, we could also not bear changing it.

I now realize that we were all traumatized, and for them, it was the compounding of primary, secondary, and tertiary trauma.

It was a mix of what happened to them, seeing what was happening to me, and what was happening to all of us:

- nationally
- historically
- generationally
- economically
- politically
- practically
- traditionally

It was our lives.

It's also important to note that it is OUR lives, everyone's lives these days. There is the collective trauma of surviving the pandemic. There is the trauma of witnessing the ravages of war internationally. Then, there is the trauma we experience in our daily lives.

No wonder so many people are tired, dejected, and counting on bandwidth or emotional capacity that does not exist.

Now that I am coming into the light, like coming out of any dark space, my eyes are straining under the weight of being seen and seeing so many others in pain.

I think my work is to continue to walk into the light, be light, and embrace my light. I am committing to seeing beyond the dark things that happened to me and standing firm in the realization that I am not the dark things that happened. Rather, I am the light that could not be consumed by them.

The Work:

1. Am I maintaining silence as a part of my trauma experience or response? If so, why? How can I cultivate and/or honor my voice in my trauma experience?

2. Can I accept compassion, empathy, or support from others when trauma has occurred? If not, why? How can I begin to allow for these reasonable responses to my trauma?

3. How can I relinquish shame, guilt, fear of rejection, or other negative emotions as I heal from trauma? Am I allowing self-blame to cloud my healing journey? Have I resorted to victim blaming? How can I center myself and my healing in this experience? What positive steps will I take to ensure that I am supported to heal wholly?

With these new insights or awareness, what commitment will I make to myself or others?

_____

_____

_____

_____

_____

Chapter 10: He Was Not the Messenger!

For years, I longed to hear him say, "I am proud of you." Although he had passed many years ago, I was still longing to hear him say I made him proud.

In many respects, there was an empty chair reserved for him at every event and milestone in my life.

I had last seen him at the age of twelve. Twelve years later, he would be murdered while administering a summer youth employment program.

While I did not know him well enough to strive to honor his legacy, I had spent much of my life striving to be good enough for him.

I am told that he advocated for children and his community. It is also said that he ran for school board and served on a commission in his community.

Years later, I am still waiting for him to serve as something that he can never be. I want him to be present. I wanted him to be affirming. I wanted him to be the man who would never leave me nor forsake me.

There are people in our lives that we hope will be the bearers of messages they were never intended to deliver. Moreover, there are messages we will seek in the eyes or words of every person we meet if we don't understand that certain messages must come from within.

While a message can be affirmed by others, it is only rooted when we know it for ourselves. Messages about our competency, efficacy, worth, and possibilities must be rooted within. When we tether these messages to other people's perceptions, they can become moving targets that feel perpetually out of reach. Moreover, in a crisis they can be shaken loose if they are not anchored in a deep sense of our own knowing.

Yesterday, a dear friend reminded me that every time I say the Lord's Prayer, I begin with "Our Father." This was profound, as I finally realized that I had been waiting for the wrong messenger.

I wanted my biological father to tell me who I was because of him. I had neglected who I was in God. I thought my biological father would tell me what my purpose was. I had ignored the ways in which I was leading a purpose-driven life in his absence.

I now know my biological father was never the intended messenger. It wasn't his message I was missing—it was the word. It was there I would discover that I was fearfully and wonderfully made. It was there I would learn that my feet were made like hind feet to walk in high places. It was there that I would learn that I was made for such a time as this.

I had the wrong messenger. With this new knowledge, I encourage others to consider if there are messages or affirmations that they may be seeking from the wrong person or tethering to the wrong place. Examples include your identity, ability, capacity, aptitude, and potential. Our parents or family can be one of the first places where we glean these messages. In the absence of them, we must be certain to develop a clear sense of them for ourselves and anchor them within. Assessments and aptitude tests can help but should never serve as the sole indicator. Our internal sense must be a litmus test.

The Work:

1. How can I develop a clear sense of self in the absence of others, external motivators, or performance?

2. Who or what am I allowing to determine my worthiness?

3. Am I attempting to perform myself into worth? Am I routinely living down to or up to other people's expectations to find satisfaction, belonging, or acceptance? Have I rooted my

identity in acts, titles, affiliations, memberships, or accolades? How can I develop a sense of self that is based on my inherent worthiness as a human being?

With these new insights or awareness, what commitment will I make to myself or others?

_____

_____

_____

_____

_____

Chapter 11: Getting Unstuck: Healing from Emotional Trauma

It can be like quicksand. The work of healing from trauma can leave you feeling like you are sinking. That's why it's critical to unpack and heal.

This weekend, I had the gift of passing by the La Brea Tar Pits. It's a well-known landmark in Los Angeles where, ages ago, herds of animals became trapped in tar and died. I am reminded of this peril, as I consider the ways we become emotionally trapped by an experience and are unable to move on emotionally.

Like tar or quicksand, we can become mired emotionally. We can contend or struggle with perceptions, our expectations, or other people's expectations in ways that leave us only sinking deeper into the abyss of our hurts.

Like herds, we can find ourselves enmeshed as families, organizations, and communities.

Our escape is contingent upon:

- a desire to be freed
- our ability to reach beyond where we are and pull ourselves forward
- our ability to hold onto and pull on something firmly rooted

So today, I am pondering these critical factors. I am asking myself and encouraging others to consider whether they really want to be free from hurt, guilt, shame, or transgressions.

You may think this answer is easy. Of course, the answer is yes.

But is it, really?

Sometimes traumas become our identity. It's like buying into being the black sheep of the family. For years, I identified as a high school dropout, even after I had four degrees.

Recently, I heard about someone who said, "They did not like me, either. They never liked me."

This person consistently rallied others who felt ostracized. It saddened me because I realize there is no amount of apology or acceptance that will ever change this narrative for this person. She has accepted being perpetually rejected as her identity in her family.

How sad!

It also compels me to consider and own the ways I am perpetually self-doubting and self-loathing. It is also compelling me to revisit if I desire to be free from how I once saw myself or felt about me.

Initially, in my anger, I wanted to call her and tell her to stop poisoning her family. Then I was forced to see that these incidents are rarely about us when they are happening. It's really about how that person sees themselves.

Similarly, how I was feeling about her behavior was not about her. It was really about me. I had been gifted an opportunity to own all the things I could control, which were:

- how I feel about it
- how I see it
- what I do about it

I am deciding to own my frustrations with her as an invitation to look inward and understand why I am sticking to certain narratives. I'm also embracing the gift of getting free by focusing on me.

As part of this evolution, I am asking how I can reach beyond our collective hurts and pull myself forward. Initially, I thought just taking the high road would suffice when I am confronted by our unresolved hurts and conflicts.

I now realize that it's like standing still in the quicksand or tar. You don't sink quickly, but you are also not out.

I have learned that when I physically or emotionally struggle with other people's hurts, traumas, or misperceptions, it only takes me deeper and faster.

What I am trying to discern is what will be freeing. Maybe it's pulling from within that frees you. Maybe it's the willingness to prioritize freeing yourself before you free others. Maybe it is accepting that you won't be able to free anyone but yourself. Maybe it is knowing that you can't free anyone who is unwilling to be unstuck. Maybe it's knowing that if a struggle ensues between the two of you while you're stuck, you will both surely perish.

I think my work this season is to focus on freeing myself.

With this conviction in mind, I am mindful of the third factor, our ability to hold onto and pull from something firmly rooted. It underscores the importance of having a firmly rooted identity.

I am actively exploring my identity. The woman I needed to be to survive is not the woman I need to be to thrive.

It's important for me to acknowledge my evolution. I must recognize the possibility that new tools, strategies, and thinking are needed for every season of my life. While some things are foundational, there is some thinking that no longer serves me. Being beholden to a black sheep identity, or beholden to shame, guilt, or rejection serves no one.

This season and every day, I free myself to love and accept myself. I free myself from the past and past hurts. I release myself from rejection. I choose a new narrative and support others to have theirs.

The Work:

1. How can I get unstuck by rooting my identity in my growth, progress, or humanity? Am I updating my perception of myself as I evolve? If not, why am I holding onto old images of myself? How am I being served by ignoring my growth? Are others served by me ignoring my growth? If so, who, how, and why? How can I shift these narratives?

2. Have I built an identity around my trauma? In what other dimensions of my experience can I ground my identity? Who am I beyond the dimensions of my trauma, like resilient or survivor? How else might I describe who I am?

3. How can I resist the temptation to struggle with others as they heal? Am I able to identify when others or myself are speaking or responding from our pain? If so, what is needed at that moment? How can I positively contribute to healing in these instances?

With these new insights or awareness, what commitment will I make to myself or others?

_____

_____

_____

_____

_____

Chapter 12: What Have You Normalized?

Have I normalized things that aren't normal?

In my coping, have I given rise to counterproductive self-destructive ways of being, thinking, and perceiving?

Did I miss or ignore my window of opportunity, the off-ramp from the chaos I no longer have to live in?

Did I forget to choose or ignore my right to choose by believing I was stuck?

Did I neglect to claim my voice, my personhood, my right to change my mind, my right to change?

Have I normalized my mistreatment by refusing to set and maintain boundaries?

Does my overlooking have me overlooked?

It's important to ask these questions, especially if we are finding that our choices no longer serve us or never did.

I am also pondering how our earliest experiences become normalized because we have no other experience or frame of reference. Moreover, I am evaluating if I have sufficiently given myself permission to:

- evolve, grow, and change
- trust
- love
- try
- make mistakes
- be different
- be ME!

I think I've taken each of these for granted. Falsely, I've assumed some of these are in conflict with:

- remembering where I come from
- being loyal
- "keeping it real"
- staying true to myself

Maybe the work is:

- being rooted but not so grounded in the past that you don't grow
- really doing better when you know better, without fearing that you will be criticized for changing or "acting different"
- having the courage to leave or the strength to stay after you have actively considered your needs
- standing in your truth, declaring your strengths, and setting boundaries without fearing you'll be perceived as "doing too much," "being extra," or "thinking you're somebody"

Either way, I think there's an opportunity to normalize:

- self-care
- balance
- boundaries
- saying no
- changing your mind
- saying I don't know
- saying I need help
- rest
- accountability
- trying
- accepting compliments and giving praise
- not participating

At different stages of my life, some, if not all, of these have not been normal.

Whether it's the way that I define humility in my faith, the enmeshment that results from family secrets and lies, or the superwoman complex, I need to carefully revisit what I have normalized.

This season, I will normalize maintaining boundaries, rest, prioritizing my needs and family, and embracing imperfection.

The Work:

1. How am I participating in or contributing to situations, relationships, and choices that do not serve me? Why am I participating?

2. How do I root out or address hidden or coercive areas of value?

3. Have I given myself permission to set and maintain boundaries? If not, how can I begin? If so, am I setting and maintaining boundaries consistently? What will I do to consistently maintain psychological safety?

With these new insights or awareness, what commitment will I make to myself or others?

_____

_____

_____

_____

_____

Chapter 13: I'm Okay

When I finally acknowledged that I was hurting, I felt pressure to be okay. Once my dark secret was out, my imperfect journey, I desperately wanted to be healed. So much so I was willing to pretend.

I wanted to put on a smile, close my eyes, and say, "I'm okay."

I wanted to rewind my sharing, edit my story, and retreat.

I deeply regretted telling.

I'm not wholly sure why.

It could've been that this truth stood in opposition to the years when someone said, "Don't tell anyone."

It might have been that I still felt unclear about why it happened to me. Partially, it was the belief that maybe I deserved it or that it could happen again. I'm not totally sure.

Some days it was defiance. It was my way of saying, "You didn't hurt me."

Either way, when I recently acknowledged that I was hurting, I really worried that I had shared too much:

- to go back
- to pretend anymore
- to continue hiding
- for the secret to be safe with me

After all, how could I acknowledge that I was hurting and live up to all the things I'm supposed to be or the things that have been said?

How could I be strong, resilient, smart, special, worthy, and be broken?

When I uttered my truth, it wasn't the deep long exhale I had envisioned. It was a choke. I immediately began choking on shame, guilt, and fear.

Divulging my truth had left me dangling. I was emotionally suspended from fears of rejection, abandonment, and judgment.

So today, this season, and however long is needed, I am declaring I'm okay.

I'm okay with however long my healing takes.

I'm okay with my scabs and the scar.

I'm okay if others can't read it or hear it. I will still say it.

I'm okay with breaking the trust of my abuser.

I'm okay if no one understands me, especially if I better understand myself.

I'm okay if my truth makes some people mad.

I'm okay if my truth makes me sad, especially if it means I'm going to be really happy one day.

I'm okay if you are uncomfortable with what I'm saying or what happened to me, especially if it means I can finally be comfortable in my skin.

I'm okay telling this ugly truth, especially if I can finally feel beautiful again.

I'm okay letting it out, cause it's freeing me too!

This season and every day forward, I'm okay.

I'm really okay!

The Work:

1. Have I accepted that what happened to me is not my fault? Can I stop taking responsibility for my abuser's choices? Can I stop blaming the victim—ME?

2. Have I forgiven myself? Am I allowing myself the grace, space, and time needed to heal? Have I acknowledged and accepted that my healing journey is unique to me and my needs?

3. How can I release myself from this undeserved guilt, shame, and fear of rejection? Have I accepted that I do not need anyone's permission to heal? Have I accepted that no penance is needed for being abused? Do I know that I don't owe anyone secrecy? Do I know that I don't need anyone's permission to tell my story?

With these new insights or awareness, what commitment will I make to myself or others?

_____

_____

_____

_____

_____

Chapter 14: Don't Forget the Inside Job!

Don't forget the inside job! It's probably the most important job we have. It definitely has the highest yield and the best compensation.

Some have said it's the work of creating happiness. Others have described it as shadow work.

As I ponder the work, I am realizing that I must stop treating it as:

- a second shift
- a side job
- a job for retirement
- a job that begins midlife
- a job only some can hold

The job of maintaining my peace, having joy, "finding myself," loving myself, and self-acceptance must be the main job!

It's the work from which everything else emanates. Things like my ability to give love begins with self-love.

Even my ability to forgive is tied to my ability to forgive myself.

If I do the work, this job, I can:

- live up to my potential
- give grace consistently
- realize my dreams
- love others
- embrace all of me
- stand in my truth
- to my own self be the truth
- be light

Most importantly, if I do this work, I can be HAPPY!

Maybe not happy every day but most days.

If I do this work, I won't have to live a life of regrets. I can begin to see my mistakes, losses, or rejections as:

- learning
- practice
- protection
- direction

I can come to the understanding that in every loss or failure, we gain things like refinement.

If I do this work, I won't:

- be worked
- overworked
- outworked
- inconsistent
- despondent

If I do this work, I can be ME—and like it!

As I begin a new season, I commit to prioritizing the inside job. I commit to making it the main work.

The Work:

1. What is my inside job? What areas of my personal development require attention? How can I begin to prioritize this development?

2. As I consider the notions of peace, self-love, acceptance, and joy, am I consistently maintaining these values? If not, why? How can I begin to address the areas that are lacking? What commitment will I make to improve these areas?

3. Am I consistently prioritizing external factors over my needs?

Do I frequently seek approval from others? Do I define success through comparison? If so, how can I begin centering more of my needs, expectations, and vision in my daily life?

With these new insights or awareness, what commitment will I make to myself or others?

_____

_____

_____

_____

_____

Chapter 15: Belonging

Sometimes, I have stayed in places, relationships, and situations longer than I should have. I stayed because I was worried about what its ending might suggest about me.

I didn't leave because leaving subtly reinforced some of my deepest fears; my fear that I was not:

- deserving
- wanted
- accepted
- needed
- enough

While human connection or belonging is a basic need, my fears exacerbated my need for belonging—so much so, that any place that would let me stay could reap the benefits of my people pleasing, proclivity to perform myself into a false sense of worth and codependency.

The result of these tendencies filtered through my skewed sense of duty and loyalty was that I lost sight of my right to ask:

- Does this work for me?
- Do I like it, you, or this?
- Is this healthy or helpful?
- How am I served by this relationship, dynamic, or these conditions?
- Do I want this?

I was so busy trying to present myself as help, a solution, or a benefit that I forgot to ask, "Does this work for me?"

After years of poor health, burnout, and dissatisfaction, I finally had to acknowledge that it wasn't working; it never did!

The trade-off was too great. It cost my identity, peace, and health. Sometimes, it even cost me:

- faith in people
- progress
- new opportunities
- healthy relationships

This year, I am redefining belonging. I will wholly embrace that it is possible to have belonging and NOT belong in:

- toxic places
- unhealthy relationships
- bad situations

Just because you want to experience belonging doesn't mean you have to:

- go with the masses
- adopt public opinion
- win a popularity contest
- go along to get along

True belonging is rooted in the following:

- self-love
- self-acceptance
- and a list of things I'm still learning

This year, I'm committing to figuring out what's on that list.

In the meantime, I'm going to revel in:

- the people who love me as I am: my husband, family, and real friends
- the places where I am "seen" and accepted

- the places that see my value
- the things that edify or fortify me
- second chances
- new opportunities

No more:

- fitting in
- hiding
- pretending
- people pleasing
- begging
- pleading
- settling
- dimming my light

This season, I remember and affirm who I am rather than being contented to just be:

- anywhere
- with anyone
- in anything

I am going to be selective.

I am going to be selective about my time, relationships, priorities, and investments.

I am also going to stop letting people choose for me or choose me without my consent.

This season and every year afterward, I will stand in the knowledge that I am chosen; therefore, I have choices, so today, I am choosing ME!

The Work:

1. How can I foster belonging in healthy ways?

2. Have I evaluated my relationships to ensure they are mutually beneficial for me and others?

3. In what ways have I rooted my sense of belonging? Is it rooted in self-love? Am I fostering a healthy sense of self-acceptance?

With these new insights or awareness, what commitment will I make to myself or others?

_____

_____

_____

_____

_____

_____

Chapter 16: The Challenge of Owning It All

I will own it all! I will own it so much that others are literally absolved of any accountability.

I will own the history of a thing even if I wasn't there.

I will own the collective failings of a thing, even if I'm only one part of the equation.

I will take this "leadership" in every area of my life. I tell myself the "buck stops here," even when it is someone else's:

- problem
- shortcoming
- mistake
- story
- journey
- opportunity
- chance
- choice
- decision

Somehow, I have conflated leading, being, and helping with being responsible for all of it.

The challenge of this belief is that it disempowers, debilitates, denies, confuses, obfuscates, and leaves me exhausted!

When I own everything, it disempowers those around me. It subtly communicates things like:

- a lack of confidence in others' ability to do something about the challenge or opportunity
- there is no role, place, or space at the table for others

- codependency and enabling are okay
- other people's opinions, perspectives, or positions don't matter

Rather than feeling empowered to change the world together, I'm left feeling resentful and unsupported, while they are left feeling unseen, underutilized, and undervalued.

It is debilitating. Over time, the weight of owning everything becomes like carrying a boulder. It begins like carrying a knapsack, but it builds.

At first, you are carrying the hurts of childhood trauma. Unfortunately, childhood trauma falsely teaches you that everything is your fault. It teaches you that you are responsible for everything around you, including other people's moods and choices. Then you take these beliefs or "responsibility" into the rest of your life.

Before you know it, you are picking up everything, including other people's problems, responsibilities, and issues. Over time, the collective weight of these things and the powerlessness you feel, because you can't change others or situations, become debilitating.

It's time for me to release this weight!

Owning it all also denies and fosters denial. When I own it all, I deny others the right to choose, act, and live as they see fit. I should not be owning what other people can do or do with their lives.

More troubling, owning it all allows me to live in a state of denial about what I can affect. If I believe and act like I have the capacity to own everything, I have subtly fallen prey to a god complex. There is no way I can be present enough, strong enough, or smart enough to own everything effectively.

It's time to live within my capacity!

Owning it all confuses me. It confuses the issue for me and others. When I own it all, without attention to whose challenge it is or my role in it, I confuse and diffuse ownership.

Consider this: Not only am I prone to confusing who should own what, but I am diffusing the ownership by "spreading it among a large number of people" or "causing it to show faintly by spreading it in many directions."

Imagine the ways that trauma, pain, and challenge are spread in families, organizations, and communities when we don't support the right people to take accountability or own their issues.

I can think of clear instances where I owned something or was forced to own something that was not mine or not wholly mine. Years or months later, I'm still apologizing or reminding myself that it was not my fault that it happened to me.

I owned my victimization as a survivor, the failure of the unemployment system, the systemic stuff that still happens structurally, institutionally, and environmentally. I even own the things that happen around me, like other people's shortcomings, choices, and failures.

Unfortunately, the owning of it all has me owning things even if:

- I wasn't there when it happened.
- I tried my best.
- It was impossible.
- It was not my fault.
- It was someone else's problem.
- Others don't want things to change.

In my emotional owning of it all, I make myself the responsible party, even when it's someone else's life, problem, or opportunity.

This is unfair to them and it is unfair to me!

Owning it all also obfuscates, "renders unclear," who should be owning the issue.

When I pick up an issue without regard for ownership, I am robbing everyone involved or enabling at best. I am robbing the owner of the opportunity to change it and the discovery of their own efficacy, agency, and ability.

I am also robbing myself of rest, peace, and partnership. In many instances, I am also enabling others and may even be trapped in a cycle of codependency. Accordingly, it's critical for me to get clear about who should be owning what.

Either way, I must acknowledge that the process of owning it all has left me exhausted at critical times in my life.

I was tired in childhood as I carried the weight of being molested. I was tired as a teenager as I carried the weight of date rape. I was tired in adulthood as I carried the weight of someone else's alcoholism.

I am tired daily from navigating the weight of pervasive isms and systemic stuff that's not mine solely to own.

I am even tired of the weight of my people pleasing and unwillingness to prioritize my needs.

This season, I'm going to own something different. I am committed to owning:

- the things I am doing to myself when I don't set and maintain boundaries.
- my life and health decisions, my priorities, and the life I want for myself.

- my role as a cheerleader, prayer partner, listening ear, sounding board, encourager, observer, or thought partner in other people's lives because I'm clear about what's mine to own and what is theirs to own.

This season and every day forward, I am going to own my stuff and empower others to own theirs by:

- respecting their decision
- supporting their vision for their life
- believing in others
- trusting God's plan and process
- giving deference
- embracing my role as a supporter
- releasing the need to fix others

This season, I release myself from the things I do not own, including people, situations, and things. This season, I also embrace everyone's right to decide and choose, even when they choose to do nothing or something different.

The Work:

1. What will I do to release the need to fix or save others?

2. How can I empower the people in my life to find their own solutions?

3. How will I set and consistently maintain appropriate boundaries?

With these new insights or awareness, what commitment will I make to myself or others?

_____

_____

_____

_____

_____

Chapter 17: Considering What I Was Given?

On my tough days, I sometimes wonder how I was given my lot.

I have asked God how He chose who I was to be in hopes that He would affirm that my existence was no mistake.

I'm certain He's not rolling dice, "grabbing a tiger by its toe," or playing best out of five.

If so, what were my odds? On my tough days, I think I would gladly trade anything for:

- a boot or a strap
- 40 acres or a mule
- a birthright
- a chance
- peace

I'll even take some privilege, in a modest dose, or a silver spoon.

On the tough days, I have lamented my experience. I have thought surely there's room for one more person to have privilege, opportunity, or hope.

As a matter of fact, I believe He has the power to change the world, so I often ask, *What are you waiting for?*

With each transgression, I have asked, *How is this my lot?*

This year, I think I have an opportunity to ask what else I was given.

Surely, I was given more than problems.

I have my mother's wit, hunger for growth, and compassion.

I have my father's gift for gab and desire for social change.

I inherited my grandmother's exacting nature. It's the foundation of my perseverance and resilience.

I have my grandfather's dutiful nature and desire for more.

I have my community's forgiving nature and unabashed commitment to hope.

I have the gift of birthing; not only people but also change.

My beauty is quietly regarded and sometimes envied.

I can literally make something from nothing like my father, my Heavenly Father.

Should I choose, I can also have peace, pride, and prosperity. I can have a positive outlook on my identity.

I think I will choose!

The Work:

1. What inherent gifts, values, talents, or assets have I been given?

2. What transgenerational lessons can I leverage or share?

3. How might my family, challenges, tragedies, or traumas affirm my resilience?

With these new insights or awareness, what commitment will I make to myself or others?

_____

_____

_____

_____

As I consider the insights and awareness gleaned from this season, what commitments to myself or others am I measuring, monitoring, and adjusting as needed, to ensure my success?

_____

_____

_____

_____

_____

_____

_____

_____

_____

_____

_____

_____

_____

_____

_____

_____

_____

_____

_____

_____

_____

_____

_____

_____

_____

_____

_____

_____

_____

_____

_____

_____

_____

_____

_____

_____

_____

_____

_____

_____

_____

Spring

My spring season brought many revelations and other key lessons. It ushered in a new dimension of acceptance. For the first time, I allowed myself to consider that things were as they were intended. When I did, I realized some things I could control. I could control how I see issues. I could control how I felt about issues. Most importantly, I could control what I did about issues.

When I remembered that I always have the ability to control my feelings, thoughts, and actions, I began exploring where I had surrendered these areas of control. What resulted were several opportunities to take back control of my life, end my hopelessness, and heal from the trauma I had ignored.

I returned to the driver's seat in my life. I was no longer a passenger in the cars of other people's trauma. Moreover, I began deciding when I would take a ride and where I was going.

Previously, I allowed myself to be hijacked or kidnapped by everyone's trauma, drama, choices, and agendas. Now I am asking myself critical questions like, *What are my expectations for this relationship, situation, and challenge?* With intention, I am choosing more often, more strategically, and from a place of ensuring that my choices serve me. As a result, a key lesson that surfaced was the importance of evaluating one's expectations. During this season, I realized the importance of examining one's expectations. As a result, I discovered I had unrealistic expectations.

Unrealistic Expectations

This awareness began with a question, *What if the problem with my past was my expectations?*

What if the people who left were never intended to stay? What if the people who never came were never intended to be there? After all, I had survived despite what I perceived as a lack of their support. This led me to another powerful question, *What if my expectations were unrealistic?*

As I followed this train of thought, I was forced to acknowledge that my expectations had been unrealistic. My expectations for a father who conceived me in an extramarital affair were unrealistic.

There I was, standing by a door emotionally and wondering why he never came to:

- raise me
- accept me
- love me
- tell me who I am
- support me
- protect me

How could he? He had failed in these areas in the place where he took his vows, in the community where he called himself a leader, and with the people who trusted him.

How could he be to me what he could not be to himself?

My expectations were too high. The few calls we had, and our encounters likely exceeded what he expected to do when he heard of my birth, and my Cosby Show fairytale about the father I should have was just that—a fairytale!

My expectations for what my mother could do alone, with her upbringing, in her community, were also unrealistic. She was a child raised in kinship care by a great-grandmother who took her in at the age of 72. This great-grandmother would pass away in my mother's senior year of high school at the age of 89. For the first time in her young life, my mother lived with her mother and became pregnant within two years at the age of 20.

Developmentally, she likely gave more than what was given to her. Transgenerationally, she gave what three generations had given. Socioeconomically, there were no acres, and there were no mules, but she provided what she could with the limited opportunities afforded her. What she gave me most was an uncommon sense of resilience.

Now, as I consider this resilience, I wonder if my expectations for myself aren't unrealistic. Maybe I'm shooting too low by expecting to tolerate or weather the challenges I face. Maybe I'm shooting too high pretending:

- Everything is okay
- That I'll "understand it by and by"
- I'm not angry and Black
- It doesn't hurt
- Code-switching isn't exhausting

Moreover, I now realize that I have been grappling with the dysmorphia of low expectations. Dysmorphia is the condition of failing to see ourselves as we are. Some describe it as an "excessive preoccupation with one's perceived flaws even when those flaws are unnoticeable to others." While it is typically a reference to flaws in one's physical appearance, I am realizing that I am obsessed with my failings, shortcomings, and nontraditional journey. Although I have overcome professional, educational, and relational challenges, I still see myself as:

- poor
- at risk
- under-resourced
- an exception
- a bastard

- incapable

Each of these is untrue.

Unfortunately, as a woman, with a diverse background, living in our society, I receive daily reminders of the possibility of becoming any one of these things. I am learning that I must shift my expectations. It is unreasonable to believe that I can not change, that things cannot change. I have already changed. My circumstances have changed.

Even if I had to begin again, I would not be starting at the same point. I would begin again with all of the learning and lessons gained from the setback. I am no longer that little girl who wondered why her father was never there. I am no longer the molested child or date rape victim. I don't have to be the mother who is still worrying and wondering if her children have made it. I am the woman making it!

Accordingly, during this season, I learned that it is critical for me to remind myself of the reality of my situation and develop self-care that enables me to maintain a healthy identity. This self-care plan includes acknowledging that I am:

- educated
- professional
- beautiful
- accomplished
- adequate
- prepared
- exceptional
- capable

While there are some that would have me believe I am a diversity hire, a statistic, and an anomaly, I must remember that I am:

- a homeowner

- a humanitarian
- a successful mother and wife
- a published researcher and author
- a leader

Most importantly, I am WORTHY!

As you consider beginning a new season, I hope you will consider the power of adjusting your expectations, telling your whole truth to others with self-forgiveness, and aligning how you see yourself with who you really are. I hope you will also consider the powerful insights that can be gleaned from the Spring reflections that follow.

Chapter 18: The Unwrapped Gift

Imagine receiving dozens of gifts on your birthday and never unwrapping them. In some respects, the unexamined life is a life of unwrapped gifts. Born with untold talents, we represent a treasure trove of realized and unrealized potential.

Consider what remains undiscovered or unopened. Have you really considered ALL that you are or bring to the table?

Do you have a reliable list of strengths, gifts, or talents that you readily leverage for purpose, provision, or actualization?

If you don't, you are likely missing:

- an opportunity to help others
- market yourself
- income streams
- a sense of accomplishment
- potential connections and relationships
- belonging

You could very well have things of utility going unused. You could have gifts that make your life and other lives better. You could be the solution!

This season, consider what you are waiting to unwrap. I recently unwrapped writing and a new level of strategy. While I had been a successful grant writer, technical writer, and published researcher, I had never written for pleasure. While witty, I have never undertaken comedic writing. While thoughtful and strategic, I had never given more than free advice. As a part of my unwrapping, I am now asking what more I hold.

This season, ask yourself:

- What comes easy to me?
- What do I do well?
- For what am I consistently sought or recognized?

The answer to these questions can be a signaling of unwrapped gifts.

Also, heed the adage, "Practice makes perfect!" Are there things you do as a hobby or in your spare time that, with practice, could become another income stream?

Don't miss the opportunity to monetize your gifts or interests. Moreover, never let fear cause you to deprive yourself or the world of your gifts.

Lastly, never let criticism, tropes, or narratives cause you to forgo using your gifts. If you are like me, you may have been on the receiving end of backhanded compliments or societal messages that caused you to dim your light.

This season, return to those moments of silencing and declare your prowess. Have you ever been asked, "Who do you think you are?"

This season, say, "I am someone powerful—I matter!"

Have you ever been asked, "What right do you have?"

This season, say, "I am deserving—I am worthy!"

Have you ever been told that you will never amount to anything?

This season, declare that you were born with infinite potential, untold gifts, and greatness on the inside—you are aptitude actualizing!

I acknowledge that this shift can be easier said than done. However, I hope others will join me on the journey of fully unwrapping who they are.

The Work:

1. What gifts have I left unwrapped?

2. What strengths, gifts, or talents can I leverage for purpose, impact, or results?

3. How can I monetize my gifts and interests?

With these new insights or awareness, what commitment will I make to myself or others?

_____

_____

_____

_____

_____

Chapter 19: You Don't Always Get to Choose, and That's Okay. Sometimes You Shouldn't!

I wear many hats. Some I chose, but many that were handed to me. This season, I am going to get clear about the hats I wear and make peace with some that were not of my choosing.

It's okay.

I chose to be a mother, a wife, and an employee in a particular company or role. Other hats were handed to me, like daughter, aunt, and niece. Whether chosen or handed, I think each is okay as long as I'm clear about my choice and ability to choose.

I can't decide to be a grandmother or a mother-in-law. Those are my children's choices and decisions. I can choose whether I will be a good one according to my capacity and healing.

I can't choose whether I will be the help, the solution, or the answer. That's not my right. The person with the problem gets to decide.

Maybe I shouldn't try to choose. Rather, I should avail myself to request and only to the extent that I can maintain balance.

I need to be clear about the ways codependence, unresolved trauma, and pain can skew my perception of choice and duty.

If I am not clear, I may fall prey to the ills of people pleasing, enabling, and projection.

I must be clear about and hold onto the knowledge that there are choices I can always have:

- I can choose how I see it.

- I can choose how I feel about it.
- I can choose what I do about it.
- I can choose to do nothing.

... but I should never choose to do everything. It's not sustainable.

I should never choose to only do it for them. They will not grow.

I should never choose to only go it alone. I will break.

I should never decide that I am all that is needed. I am not God.

Realizing that:

- I'm not God.
- It's only helpful if it feels helpful to the person with the problem.
- I can't change people, and I shouldn't try.

I think the work for me this season is to accept and make the change that I can, when desired, when received, and only if it empowers others to be their solution in the long run. Anything more or less than this is robbing me of my choice or someone else of their choice.

The Work:

1. How can I honor my right to choose? How can I honor other people's right to choose? How can I work to ensure these rights coexist?

2. Where might I falsely be surrendering my right to choose? From what principle, expectation, belief, or trauma might I be surrendering? How can I shift this area of challenge?

3. Where might I be overstepping others' right to choose? From what need, fear, or expectation may I be exerting my will on others? What will I do to shift this practice?

With these new insights or awareness, what commitment will I make to myself or others?

_____

_____

_____

_____

_____

Chapter 20: Idling?

Are you idling?

Are there places in your life where you have made a decision but you haven't taken action?

Are there instances when you have committed to a new vision for your life, but you feel stuck in your old ways, patterns of being, or relegated to the status quo?

Apathy, stagnation, or inaction can be shame-inducing. If you have started the shame spiral of "should-ing" on yourself by saying things like, "I should have been done by now," let's interrupt it!

Let's pivot from idling to action!

One of the most powerful ways to overcome inaction is by taking action. I know this can be easier said than done, but let's do it by taking a few key steps together:

1. Brainstorm a list of steps or tasks that can contribute to accomplishing your goal.
2. Organize the steps or tasks from easiest to most difficult.
3. Review each step to determine which can be accomplished alone and which require support from others.
4. Select one task or step you can accomplish alone in the next 48 hours.
5. Put the step or task on your daily To-Do list for the next 72 hours or until completed within those 72 hours.

If you do not complete the task within the next 72 hours, please respond to and rule out the following internal constraints:

- Do I believe the goal is possible? If so, what steps or tasks on my list will make it a reality?
- Do I believe I am deserving of achieving this goal?
- Have I committed to prioritizing my needs each week?

If the answer is no to any of these questions, let's get to a yes by:

1. Affirming your worth through repeating a daily affirmation for 21 days.
2. Writing down an actionable vision for your goal; be sure to describe how it will look, sound, and feel when you accomplish it.
3. Including yourself on your daily To-Do list for the next 21 days.

As with most things, our ability to achieve a goal begins with having a clear vision, plan, and sense of worth that says we are deserving of achieving our goals.

If you are idling, begin by taking one next step. This step can be small, and it can even be done using the above-mentioned strategies.

As someone who had to rule out all of the questions above and leveraged the strategies to complete a dissertation, 19 publications, four education programs, and 22 years of grant writing, I can attest to the power of these strategies and getting clear about the questions.

Join me in moving from idling to action!

The Work:

1. Have I clearly defined my goals? If so, have I done the work to ensure they become more than wishes? Have I empowered them to be a daily compass for thoughts, actions, and feelings?

2. Have I developed and implemented a plan of action to achieve my goals? Have I empowered this plan to be a roadmap or daily guide for my choices, preferences, and actions?

3. Am I taking steps to meet my goals? Each day? Each week? Each month? Am I ensuring that results are in alignment with my desired goals? Am I allowing for revisions, course corrections, rerouting, or detours to ensure I remain headed in the right direction?

With these new insights or awareness, what commitment will I make to myself or others?

_____

_____

_____

_____

_____

Chapter 21: Stuck in Labor

Don't get stuck in labor! If the thing you are birthing is crowning, it is time to push. An unwillingness to push will only result in the death of your dream.

While not a literal death, it will be the death of your aspiration and the death of the thing you were to give to the world.

Should you fail to push, it will also be the death of your confidence, sense of self-efficacy, and others' hopes.

So, push!

Push beyond your need to know that it will be perfect, that you are enough, and that all will be well.

Don't let your worries about being great or adequate cause you to lose sight of the fact that you are in labor.

Remember, the nature of labor is that you have reached the gestational capacity of the womb where your dreams began.

Just as there is an inherent relationship between gestation and birthing, there is a divine timing underway that should not be delayed. Our dreams can only be held within us for so long lest they die.

If you have been holding your breath, resisting an internal push to do or become, or refusing to deliver, it is time for you to take a deep breath, bear down, and push!

This may mean starting the business, investing in the dream, finishing the book, buying the house, or starting your next chapter. Whatever you are to birth, know that it can't remain in the birthing canal. You can't sustain perpetual holding, and it can't be sustained by you perpetually holding onto fear, doubt, or shame.

This season, allow your "it" to come to fruition!

The Work:

1. What am I intended to birth?

2. How am I pushing myself to deliver?

3. What may be gained if I relinquish my fears and fully commit to my vision?

With these new insights or awareness, what commitment will I make to myself or others?

_____

_____

_____

_____

_____

Chapter 22: Reclaiming

Have you left your identity, dreams, or sense of the possibilities in an old place or the wrong place?

While participating in a meditative practice, I realized I had left my hopes with my last lesson.

Sometimes, when we experience failure, we believe our dreams and aspirations die, too. We begin to foreclose on our possibilities.

In the moment, these failures can feel catastrophic. However, we must remember that nothing can be honed without practice. Trial and error are fundamental parts of progress, success, and achievement.

Consider the number of attempted shots, touchdowns, goals, or swings that are a part of any win. Now, consider the number of attempts that make up any championship or sports dynasty. It is the willingness to try again that fosters success.

So this week, try again!

Identify one thing you want to achieve and take the next step.

Revisit the last attempt and tweak something.

Identify someone doing what you want to do and get their advice.

Fill in your knowledge or skill gap with a coach, a book, a mentor, or practice.

It doesn't have to be everything you need to get there. You can start with just one thing!

So tomorrow, start with one thing, and each day, make it one more. Before you know it, you will be there.

One of my greatest failings was leaving school in the wake of my assault. Not only had my assailant taken my innocence, but I had allowed him to take my will and hopes.

I am proud to say that not only did I reclaim my will to live, but I also earned my high school diploma and four degrees by "trying again." Those degrees and diplomas were a culmination of many drafts, quizzes, tests, retests, and a whole lot of practice.

With this initial failure and others in mind, I am mindful of the importance of returning to the scene of my losses and claiming the lessons they offer. I am also mindful of the critical need to ensure that I reclaim my hopes, my identity, and the possibilities in the wake of failure. It is almost always the case that something is possible. However, nothing will be possible if we don't try again.

This season, I am trying again, and I hope you will, too!

The Work:

1. What might I reclaim if I revisit my strategy or approach to my last challenge?

2. Where might I find a new opportunity, gift, or approach if I revisited my failings?

3. What will I do to ensure that I "try again?"

With these new insights or awareness, what commitment will I make to myself or others?

_____

_____

_____

Chapter 23: Unlearning as a Winning Strategy

Our ability to unlearn is as critical as our ability to learn. Defined as "the ability to discard false or outdated information or bad habits," unlearning is a vital part of progress.

During this year of reflection, I am actively evaluating my beliefs and resisting the temptation to neatly categorize people, seasons, or situations.

This can be easier said than done when you don't take the time to rest and reflect. Moreover, if you are a workaholic, you have likely come to rely on some categorizations that may not be reliable.

Here are a few things I am unlearning this week:

- finishing my plate
- filling silence with words
- asking for permission
- waiting my turn

Initially, this unlearning felt counterintuitive. After much reflection, I don't know how I sustained some of these counterproductive practices. For example, I have been striving to finish my plate no matter what others put on it. Moreover, I readily allowed others to put anything on my plate, including their needs, problems, and expectations. Imagine trying to finish a plate that is readily filled with other people's stuff. I'm no longer finishing that plate.

I also had a habit of filling other people's silence with words. Even more troubling, I treated every pregnant pause as an opportunity to birth a solution or suggestion, or offer help. Rather than give others the time and space they needed to decide what to do, I readily offered to save, help, or do. Moreover, I would become increasingly resentful when they did not treat my support as modeling. Imagine thinking that you've shown someone what to do and realizing that you are doing it for them, and they didn't even ask you to do it. Suffice it to say, I am now considering how to pivot from enabling to empowering others by listening.

I am also done asking for permission to:

- change my mind
- grow
- shine
- set boundaries
- say no

None of these decisions require anyone's permission but mine! I don't know why I ever asked, but I'm done asking for permission in these areas.

Lastly, I'm done with waiting my turn to:

- be happy
- fulfilled
- rest
- stop
- begin

I relinquish how I have defined "my turn." My turn is no longer contingent upon anyone else's turn, convenience, or needs.

This season, I unlearn anything that places me last in my own life!

The Work:

1. As I consider the practices, thinking, and feelings that no longer serve me, what can I commit to unlearn?

2. When needed, am I giving myself permission to change, grow, or go? If not, why? How can I shift this faulty approach?

3. Am I waiting to be happy, whole, and healed? How can I stop delaying my growth? Have I done the work to understand when to pivot, change course, or adjust?

With these new insights or awareness, what commitment will I make to myself or others?

_____

_____

_____

_____

_____

Chapter 24: Love in the Absence of Self

My prayer today is that we fully allow ourselves to experience the love waiting for us.

May we have the love that happens in wholeness and peace—the peace of knowing we are deserving.

May we release any hurt or experience standing in the way of the unconditional love that we can have when we shed our fears, trust our hope, and move forward in faith.

May we realize and express more deeply the love that is unrelenting, unconditional, and transforming.

May we come to know the love that empowers, transcends, and abides.

May we begin to meet in the middle those who seek to love us because we have finally realized how we ask them to traverse:

- the distance left by absent fathers and mothers
- the emotional roads traveled in grief
- the unyielding expectations fostered by the fairytale
- the walls that must be mounted in the wake of generational pathology
- the resolution and apology that never came
- the hole or hurt left by the first breakup, divorce, or past infidelity

May we embrace the love that cleaves and is long-suffering enough to drown out our fears.

May we know what it is to be the apple of someone's eye because we embrace what we see in the mirror.

May we wholly love because we have finally attained wholeness.

May you begin with the love that is just the three of you:

- me,
- myself,
- and I.

May you finally come to the recognition that love in the absence of self-love is fleeting.

May we have the courage to heal so we can:

- hold onto and live from the best parts of ourselves
- uplift others
- speak a kind word
- trust
- love unconditionally
- hope again

May we finally love in the absence of our fears so we may love ourselves and love others.

The Work:

1. What declaration of love can I make today?

2. How can I begin the practice of loving myself and others in ways that empower me to realize self-acceptance?

3. What do I mean when I say I love myself?

With these new insights or awareness, what commitment will I make to myself or others?

_____

_____

_____

_____

_____

Chapter 25: Do We Confuse Our Knowing?

Sometimes, I think I confuse my knowing with the duty to change things. Falsely, I have believed that I could change a person, a place, or a situation because I believed it could be better or should be different.

What is happening in the moments when we are tempted to say things like:

- If only you would...
- Why can't you just...
- All you have to do is...

Whatever is happening, we have an opportunity to consider if our need to do something or fears about imperfection have led us down the false path of believing we know best. We must be aware of the potential to minimize the experience of others, and everyone's right to choose.

This awareness is compelling me to revisit some critical roles in my life like mother, leader, and advocate. As a mother of ADULT children, do I really know best?

As a leader, can I really change things through examples if I'm not modeling? How am I deciding when advocacy is needed? Maybe I have missed the opportunity to just hold space.

As I begin another season, I am committing to being clear about the role of my knowing, certain I really know, and fostering a climate that supports everyone's journey of knowing!

The Work:

1. Am I frequently offering unsolicited advice? Do I treat everyone's problems as a call to action? Am I case-managing the people in my life? If so, how can I pivot from enabling others to empowering others to find solutions?

2. Am I avoiding my problems by focusing on other people's problems? Am I working harder on other people's issues than my own issues? Am I delaying my progress to help others reach their goals? If so, how can I center my needs more in my daily efforts?

3. Who or what is served when I delay, deny, or distract from my progress?

With these new insights or awareness, what commitment will I make to myself or others?

_____

_____

_____

_____

_____

Chapter 26: Authorship

Sometimes, we allow others to shake our confidence, shape our identity, and shift our priorities.

In these moments, we must acknowledge this "authorship" and ensure that its resulting narrative, aims, and efforts align with the vision we have for ourselves. We must be conscious of our surrendering of the pen and cognizant of the chapter underway.

While purging and organizing today, I became painfully aware of my own surrender and the ways I have forgotten who I am. In reclamation, I began reading cards that I have received over the years, cards that speak to my nature, character, disposition, impact, and priorities.

I encourage anyone who is wondering who they are or if they "walk their talk" to do a self-check.

Some questions I am asking myself today and encourage others to consider are:

- What evidence do I have for how I am feeling or fearing?
- Who is deciding who I am, who I get to be in this moment and what I will become?
- Who is the author and finisher of my life or story?
- What or who is served by the state I am in?
- Am I in agreement with how this makes me feel, how I am choosing to respond and the resulting outcomes?

As I began listing what evidence there was for how I was feeling, I realized I had surrendered authorship. I was letting things external to me write my narrative or story. The chapter underway was not consistent with who I know myself to be. In some instances it had literally shaken my knowing.

The cards I reread today not only affirmed who I could be, but they reminded me of who I am.

This season, I will reclaim my story. When I am shaken, I will stand in the truth of who I have demonstrated myself to be:

- "enjoyed partnership and accomplishments created through your leadership"
- "endless support of staff"
- "managing different work styles comes naturally"
- "you bring joy, positivity, and light into the office every day"
- "you treat employees with dignity and grace"
- "others will strive to honor your legacy"
- "tremendous heart and spirit for the work is unmatched"
- "support and cheer us on"
- "positive attitude and kindness"
- "work to make the team better"
- "passion for doing the right thing and having difficult conversations inspires others"
- "lead by example and fearlessly"
- "example of what a leader can do to inspire and make an impact"
- "missed smile and laughter"
- "wisdom and thoughtfulness"
- "help children succeed"
- "vision for improving services"
- "inspiring leadership"
- "make the community a better place"
- "under your leadership, I am seeing myself grow"
- "fierce advocate for change"
- "unwavering community commitment"
- "obvious passion for the work"
- "dedicated public servant"

- "drive and passion to change the world for all humankind"
- "role model"
- "we are no longer invisible"
- "reach back and lend a helping hand"

I also want to underscore the critical importance of periodically reminding yourself of your gifts, aptitude, talents, and achievements. Moreover, in toxic environments, unhealthy relationships, and moments of uncertainty, it is imperative that you revisit the questions above and things, like your:

- why
- strengths
- purpose
- calling
- examples of resilience
- possibilities
- promise

Lastly, please consider joining me in reclaiming or holding onto the things that matter, like your:

- peace
- identity
- hope
- faith

This Work:

1. Who is deciding who I am, who I get to be in this moment, and what I will become?

2. What or who is served by the state I am in?

3. If needed, how can I reclaim, recapture, or refocus to ensure a vision and life of my making?

With these new insights or awareness, what commitment will I make to myself or others?

_____

_____

_____

_____

_____

Chapter 27: Use the Membership

This season, I'm pushing myself to use my memberships.

In something akin to a gym membership, there are places where I have joined, but I have yet to fully realize or use all of my benefits. I have allowed fear, doubt, and old narratives to preclude me from realizing the gifts I have in my relationships, talents, and network.

Are you fully realizing the benefits of the memberships you hold?

Have you signed onto "for better, for worse, for richer, for poorer, in sickness and in health" but allowed old narratives and other people's hurts to stop you from relying on your partner?

Do you have a network of friends and supporters, but rarely allow them to see when you are in need or hurting?

Do you have a family with a rich legacy of resilience, but spend most of your time pretending everything is okay?

Do you have gifts and talents, but allow fear and doubt to prohibit you from fully realizing your potential?

If you said yes to any of these questions, you have an opportunity to explore why you are consciously or unconsciously living below your potential.

This season, I encourage you to consider the places and spaces where you have committed to membership but have yet to fully realize the benefits. Address limiting beliefs, release fear, and fully inhabit the relationships, partnerships, and resources you have been given. Embrace interdependence as an inherent dimension of independence.

Allow yourself to be fully supported, loved, and accepted. Use all of your gifts, not just the familiar, generally accepted, practiced gifts. Choose to bring yourself fully to your marriage, friendships, and goals.

This season, fully take hold of the benefits of membership!

The Work:

1. Where do I have memberships that have gone unused? Why have they gone unused? How can I begin to use them?

2. Am I allowing myself to be supported by others? If not, why? What needs to shift for me to accept love, support, or acceptance from others?

3. Have I brought myself fully to my marriage, friendships, or goals? If not, why? How can I begin to be fully present in these relationships or priorities?

With these new insights or awareness, what commitment will I make to myself or others?

_____

_____

_____

_____

_____

Chapter 28: Watching Your Step

It's critical to go beyond watching your steps to seeing your steps.

If you are a failing perfectionist like me, you have likely been watching your step all your life. You probably spend a great deal of time:

- calculating the next step
- watching your step as though navigating a minefield
- rethinking your steps after taking them

This can be debilitating!

What if you were able to see your steps instead of watching them?

How might your perspective change if you saw your step as:

- a vehicle instead of a risk
- a natural part of progress
- a prerequisite to success

How might your experience of your journey change if you acknowledged that missteps, two steps backwards, and overstepping are inevitable as you practice your footing?

If you spend an inordinate amount of time walking on eggshells, second-guessing yourself, or hyper-vigilantly watching your step, you have an opportunity to begin trusting yourself and trusting the journey.

This may feel easier said than done, so it's critical to remember your steps have:

- kept you alive!
- you positioned to have another tomorrow! You are getting through today!
- taken you to some heights and out of some lows!

Also, remember that your steps can be adjusted as needed!

Over the course of my professional and personal journey, I've taken many steps. Some steps were unsure. Some steps were repeated. Sometimes, I stepped over things. Still, other times, I wondered if I had overstepped.

What I have come to know as I pivot from watching my steps to seeing my steps is that each step has made me better in some way.

The unsure ones taught me that I could trust myself when they worked out. The repeated ones taught me that I had a path forward or out if I needed one. The baby steps taught me that I could pace myself or go as slow as I needed. The big steps taught me that I could make up ground or change my situation in the blink of an eye.

Now that I can see my steps instead of watching them, my steps are teaching me that I can get to wherever I desire.

May you begin to see your steps, too! See all the places they have taken you and all the places you can go!

The Work:

1. How can I reframe my steps to acknowledge my resilience?

2. What are some steps I can take to manage my pacing?

3. How can I acknowledge each of the steps along the path of my journey and affirm their value?

With these new insights or awareness, what commitment will I make to myself or others?

_____

_____

_____

_____

_____

Chapter 29: They Didn't Corner Your Market! Your Corner Is Empty!

Recently, I had a powerful conversation with two of my dearest friends. We were exploring what becomes of the missed opportunity. One friend lamented having a powerful book concept and later seeing a similar publication.

As she shared, we were each reminded that whatever is for you is truly for you. The thing you are called to do, you can and will do should you decide.

Just as shirts come in many styles, colors, shapes, and seasons, your calling will come in a unique shade of you.

No other person can deliver you. Even when others replicate, duplicate, or emulate, there's still the you that is uniquely you and the calling that is uniquely yours!

I liken it to every burger chain that has emerged since the first burger chain. They each entered the market, knowing there were others but believing there was a place for their chain.

In concert, one friend exclaimed, "They can't corner your market! Your corner is empty. It will be empty till you come, but recognize that the world is waiting!"

If you are worried that you have procrastinated your way out of the possibility, begin. Begin with the knowledge that even when there are similarities, there's a difference only you can make. So be the first person to:

- make your sauce
- tell your story

- coin your term
- design your line
- do it your way

Boldly stand in you and do the thing you are called to do. Just as there are many brands of one product, solutions to the same problem, cures for the same disease, and a plethora of hamburger recipes, there is room for you!

May you be empowered to deliver on that nagging desire, persistent promise, and enduring idea!

The Work:

1. What idea, product, service or vision am I delaying delivering?

2. Why am I delaying? Have I embraced that I am worthy, capable and deserving of delivering? Are there hidden beliefs at play that are causing me to delay manifesting the vision I have been given?

3. How can I take action now? What steps will I take to achieve my vision? How will I consistently prioritize taking action toward delivering?

With these new insights or awareness, what commitment will I make to myself or others?

_____

_____

_____

_____

_____

Chapter 30: Know Your Assignment

If you have ever spent time trying to change how someone else acts, thinks, or feels by changing yourself, you have missed the assignment.

The desire to change others by changing yourself is an indication that you are doing the wrong work.

Falsely, I believed that I could change others by taking responsibility for their intentions, beliefs, feelings, and actions.

In something akin to taking medicine and expecting the other person to get better, I was willing to change how I showed up in hopes that others would change their perspective, intentions, or behavior.

This false premise is a recipe for people pleasing, enabling, and trauma. If you are responding to other people's poor behavior, bad intentions, or bias by making excuses, making exceptions, or making up without an apology and changed behavior, your assignment is to understand why.

Contrary to popular belief, people are not changed by your example. They are changed by their decision to adopt your example. If we are to successfully change anything, it is ourselves!

Our assignment is to acknowledge and hold steadfast to:

- setting and maintaining healthy boundaries
- remembering our worth, happiness, and peace are inside jobs
- knowing that people are not our assignments or projects

Only when we consistently do the work of operating from these principles are we empowered to change our conditions. This is the assignment.

The Work:

1. How can I consistently set and maintain healthy boundaries?

2. What am I doing to affirm my worth, maintain happiness, and sustain peace in my daily life?

3. How can I disrupt the cycle of codependency, enmeshment, and people pleasing in my life? How will I identify that it is occurring and act to disrupt it?

With these new insights or awareness, what commitment will I make to myself or others?

_____

_____

_____

_____

_____

Chapter 31: What Are You Sticking To?

One great epiphany that came from my processing is that I need to make the shift from feeling stuck to realizing I am sticking. So, as I begin a new season, I am asking, "What am I sticking to?"

Have I been feeling stuck but really just sticking to:

- old ways of doing things?
- old mindsets?
- old narratives?
- old familiar people and places?

If you have been sticking to some things that have you feeling stuck, please join me in doing something new this new season. May your season be filled with new adventures, gifts, relationships, opportunities, and perspectives!

The Work:

1. To what familiar patterns or practices am I sticking? How did these patterns or practices previously serve me? Why do they no longer serve me? What new patterns or practices will I replace with them?

2. What thinking, mindset, philosophy, or beliefs are making it difficult to move forward? How can I reframe them to achieve the goals or life I want?

3. What people or places are hindering my growth? Why am I maintaining these relationships or continuing to go to these places? What need or needs are these relationships or places serving in my life? How does maintaining my engagement negatively impact me? What could I gain if I released them or the need? What will I do to change today?

With these new insights or awareness, what commitment will I make to myself or others?

_____

_____

_____

_____

_____

Chapter 32: Let It Take Root!

Once you begin the journey inward, you will discover many opportunities for change. Six months into my journey, I discovered an opportunity to grow in every area of my life. If I am not careful to manage my expectations for growth, I could be pushed into paralysis. So, this season, I am unpacking the need for change through reflection.

As a result, I have decided to focus my efforts by taking on a little change at a time. Today, I am committing to letting something take root!

As a first step, I decided to review all of my reflections and determine what opportunities for change were reflected. By the end of the third month, I had filled a page.

Broadly, there were things like "change how I see myself," so I listed steps I could take, like changing my hairstyle, updating my wardrobe, getting a new headshot, changing my purse, or changing how I receive compliments. I also noted things like updating my resume, redoing my bio, identifying my brand, listing and living my values, and changing my self-talk.

Other opportunities that manifested were things like maintaining healthy relationships, boundaries, and expectations. As I unpacked what this declaration meant, every relationship in my life was under consideration.

It compelled me to revisit so many fundamental aspects of my life, such as what friendship is, how I can be a good adult daughter and the mother of adult children, and where my principles for marriage come from.

Even more profoundly, I began exploring my expectations for myself. I asked myself why I don't defend myself sometimes and why I so readily defend others. The complexity of not standing up for myself while always taking a stand for justice made me unpack whether I believed I was worthy. It also compelled me to consider how effective I could be at love without self-love.

By the time I reviewed my first quarter of reflections, I had to stop and breathe. I thought to myself, I could easily birth a new person at the end of this year of reflection.

Was I ready for the labor that would entail?

After much thought, I have decided to let something take root.

Instead of trying to change something every time something comes up, I am changing one thing at a time, during a quarter, for this year.

I am giving myself the time to understand my "why" and choose "how" I want to proceed. Most importantly, I am giving myself the practice and grace I need to see "what" works.

I am letting this powerful transformation take root!

The Work:

1. What changes am I seeking and why?

2. How might I prioritize the desired changes? Which changes will I make first? Are there changes that require my immediate attention?

3. Am I prioritizing changes that require effort from others? How can I prioritize changes that are manageable, attainable, and realistic? What resources are needed to make and sustain my desired changes? What action will I take today?

With these new insights or awareness, what commitment will I make to myself or others?

_____

_____

_____

_____

_____

Chapter 33: Let

I'm going to start "letting" so I can live.

I'm going to start with "letting" myself do "it"—whatever "it" is—right NOW.

There is no better time than right now to start living!

Falsely, I have assumed there will always be time.

I don't know what watch I was checking, but my newest awareness is that we really don't know if we will have time to:

- get it right
- do it later
- say it when we're ready
- ignore it
- pretend
- participate in things that don't serve us
- be in relationships that harm us
- accept or tolerate much of anything that isn't good for us

Our time in this world is unknown.

I don't want to wake up and realize that I spent one minute too much self-sabotaging, self-harming, or self-destructing.

I don't want to give another minute to hurtful people, situations, or things!

I don't want to wait for permission anymore, permission to:

- speak my peace
- tell my truth
- live authentically

- love and accept myself
- be happy
- have boundaries or hope

I just don't have time!

I really never did! Especially if the thing I've been choosing between is my and everyone else's desires, needs, and wants.

I don't have another minute to not choose ME!

So, I am going to "let."

If need be, I am going to:

- let the chips fall where they may
- let go
- let my "no" be a complete sentence
- let myself cry, feel it, and release it
- let myself go first
- let myself do it right now
- let "it" pass, go by, or end if it means jeopardizing my safety, peace, or health
- let love in
- let other people help or support me
- let myself think about it before I decide
- let myself be fully present and hopeful
- let me down from the cross
- let them go on without me
- let God have his perfect way
- let the process work

I'm just going to let!

This season, I will let myself have health, peace, and an uncommon kind of love, self-love!

The Work:

1. What am I going to let go to have the life I want?

2. What am I going to let happen so I may move forward?

3. How has letting anything happen harmed me? How can I be more intentional about my choices, relationships, and efforts?

With these new insights or awareness, what commitment will I make to myself or others?

_____

_____

_____

_____

_____

Chapter 34: Give Yourself Space

This season and everyday forward, I am committed to giving myself the space I need to show up as my best, most informed, present self.

This season, I consciously choose to diffuse the triggers that would have me respond from:

- fear
- duty
- anger
- hopelessness
- anxiety

Those emotions or expectations do not serve me.

They leave me people pleasing, working to burnout, hurting, shaming, spiraling in guilt, apathetic, complacent, feeling inadequate, saving and trying to be someone else's hope, guarded, defensive, depressed, or anxious.

If I'm not careful, I'll even begin to learn helplessness. Accordingly, this season and every day forward, I choose to be:

- healed: no longer responding from the broken places of my past, other people's trauma or expectations, or the need to be perfect
- trusting: trusting that I am capable, worthy and deserving of wins, peace, joy and love
- rested: well poised to succeed because I have taken care to rest; rest my body while resting in the knowledge that I am enough
- whole: wholly present in my life, choosing from conscious places, and leveraging the best of myself

- graceful and grace giving: taking care in my actions while readily extending to others the things I need like patience, care, acceptance, and love
- centered and grounded: centered and grounded in the knowledge that I was intended, God is never surprised, and I will and am making it
- purposeful: acting with intention and careful consideration of the impact, implications, and my desire to empower and inspire

This season and anytime I feel overwhelmed, undervalued or thwarted, I will remember to trust the process is working. I will believe things are happening for me, not to me. I will remember my strengths and accept my limitations as a reflection of God's divine authorship.

I will live by the knowledge that:

"And we know that all things work together for good to them that love God, to them who are the called according to his purpose. For whom he did foreknow, he also did predestinate to be conformed to the image of his Son, that he might be the firstborn among many brethren. Moreover, whom he did predestinate, them he also called: and whom he called, them he also justified: and whom he justified, them he also glorified." Romans 8:28-30 KJV

I repeat:

This too is working for your good and mine. Knowing that we have been called to this moment together, with my love for him and desire to be who He would have me be to you and others, I gently remind myself that:

- He knew me from my conception; literally before my journey even began; He knew I would have these strengths, limitations and desires, and it was well with Him!

- I was predestined; crafted with intention and purpose; I am not a mistake; this is my season!
- I am called and predestined to realize and achieve all that He has intended for me, He has justified my journey; a justification that can be found in every twist and turn I have taken, my highs and lows, and a journey that is still unfolding
- He justified who I am and all I would do, he also glorified; He is proud of me and takes pleasure in me trying, doing my best with what I have, and growing

In the moments when I am triggered by the things that have not changed or will not change, I will give myself space.

The Work:

1. What will I do to ensure that I am not choosing from negative triggers?

2. How will I act to embrace the belief that all things are working for my good?

3. What can I do to center peace, abundance, clarity, and wholeness in my daily life?

With these new insights or awareness, what commitment will I make to myself or others?

_____

_____

_____

_____

_____

Chapter 35: Live and Let Live

Instead of doing New Year's resolutions, I committed to a year of processing. The vulnerability and transparency have been uncomfortable and scary at times. I have considered not sharing or even pretending that my journey is perfect. I've also wanted to defend or protect my family by underscoring that I am not talking about them.

Tonight I'm overcoming my fears about judgment and sharing something I've been processing for a few weeks. Frankly, I'm still processing it, but I'm going to share it because I think it will help someone. If you are an empath or a trauma survivor, I believe you will appreciate someone articulating the feeling that you have to own everything or carry the weight of other people's feelings and actions. I hope this reflection blesses you:

Before I had children or married, the notion of "live and let live" was easy to support and do.

It sounds great in theory, but the practice can be daunting.

As a mother, wife, family member, and employee, I sometimes struggle with the decisions that are made around me, for me, or for others; especially when I believe someone's well-being is at stake.

Everyone in my life is an adult empowered to make their own decisions, including my children, my husband, my parent—everyone!

I am a mom, but I don't get to make my adult children do anything. Even when I thought I was the boss, they were really acquiescing.

I am a wife, and most, if not all, of our decisions are made by consensus and only to the extent that we each feel seen, heard, and respected.

I have been hired by boards to head organizations, a governor to head a system, a city to manage work, and even in these roles I alone can't change a culture or climate.

Publicly, I say live and let live, but privately I'm on pins and needles, walking on eggshells and biting my fingernails as I watch decisions be made each day by others that aren't the decisions I would make.

I want to say things like "I wouldn't do that if I were you," to which others rightly reply:

- "But you are not me!"
- "You are not the boss of me!"
- "Who asked you?"

Gently, they sometimes say, "There's more than one way to skin a cat."

Inside, I retort:

- "You don't have to make this mistake. You can learn from other people's mistakes."
- "You don't have to make this mistake, you can learn from my mistake."
- "You don't have to make this mistake. Don't repeat history!"

Then quietly, I remind myself:

- things are happening for me, not to me
- to trust the process
- it's not my life

Still, somewhere in the darkness or background, are the faint whispers:

- "Why is this happening?"
- "How did I cause this?"
- "What could I have done differently?"

- "What did I do wrong?"

As I write this, I realize that part of my challenge is that I feel personally responsible for what others decide and the impact of their decisions.

Sadly, I have been emotionally owning other people's stuff all my life, and it's exhausting. I have spent most of my life apologizing. I apologize for others and their behavior. I apologize for other people's abuse. I apologize for what happens in marginalized communities and tone-deaf societies. I apologize for setting and maintaining boundaries. I apologize for crying or feeling bad about the atrocities that happened. I apologize for being right sometimes and wrong for others. I even apologize for being upset cause I can't be angry, black, and female—that's not allowed.

I have also spent most of my life covering. I cover so others don't feel bad. I keep family secrets and lies. I pretend that everything is okay. I pretend that things are not happening. I pretend things didn't happen. I cover with forgiveness the transgressions that broke my heart, my spirit, and my peace. I even cover other people's backs, including the people who never have mine.

Even today, I am managing. I am managing the climate, culture, moods, attitudes, and people around me through debilitating practices like:

- code-switching
- pretending not to see the pink elephant in the room
- wearing a mask
- dimming my light
- numbing
- going along to get along

I also take the high road no matter how heartbreaking, heart-wrenching, disheartening, concerning, troubling, or abusive the behavior I am subjected to managing becomes.

This season, I release myself from owning other people's decisions, moods, attitudes, mistakes, and choices.

I am also committing to setting and maintaining boundaries. When personal accountability, social responsibility, shared accountability, being my brother's keeper, a member of the village, and my other roles collide, I am allowed to feel tired, exhausted, and even hopeless. Accordingly, I am committing to maintaining balance. I'm going to get clear about doing what I can, when I can, to the extent that I can, without guilt.

Acknowledging the weight can feel so great that I don't feel at all, I'm also committed to not being in denial. I will no longer deny the emotional toll of the atrocities, inconsistencies, discrepancies, ideologies at play, or the psychology of managing personal health.

I am going to do the work!

Minimally, I am committing to remembering:

- I can only change myself.
- I can only manage myself.
- I can only be responsible for myself.

Accordingly, I will not make myself emotionally responsible for everyone and everything around me. That is a trauma response that no longer serves me. This trauma response only serves to reinforce feelings of powerlessness and despondency.

With a commitment to living an empowered life, I free myself from owning anything other than myself. Moreover, I commit to not being owned by other people's choices, decisions, behaviors, and feelings.

This season and every day forward, I will maintain boundaries that allow me to love and take care of myself while empowering others to do the same.

The Work:

1. Am I owning things that don't belong to me? If so, why? Who or what does this serve? How can I center my needs, areas of influence, and experience more in my living?

2. Am I treating every issue or problem I observe as a call to action? Am I exhibiting a savior complex? Am I attempting to be God in other people's lives?

3. Am I codependent in one or more areas of your life? Am I enmeshed in my family or other relationships? How can I identify and maintain healthy boundaries?

With these new insights or awareness, what commitment will I make to myself or others?

_____

_____

_____

_____

_____

Chapter 36: Drive!

Instead of letting the things that trouble me drive me crazy, I'm going to let them drive me to change!

There is a price I pay for complacency, apathy, and paralysis.

Rather than saving myself a headache, I pay for these things in my physical and emotional health.

It's the cost of swallowing, silencing, and inaction.

I pay a toll to swallow my emotions, silence my voice, and look the other way.

It's the price of the bystander who refuses to act. They silently teach themselves and others that no one will come to their aid when they are in distress.

It's the way that we perpetuate silence until we are silenced.

It's the way I support abuse when I won't defy the abuser. I teach all of us that it's okay, we are deserving of it, and there is no recourse.

This season, I will not let troubles, troubling people, or troubling situations drive me. I will drive!

I'm putting myself back in the driver's seat of my life by changing:

- my response
- my perspective
- my position

No more sucking it up. I'm done drinking this bad mix, this cocktail of indecision, this recipe for inadequacy.

You are not the boss of me, Trouble!

I will not be driven to extremes, driven to depression, or driven to inaction.

As a matter of fact, I'm going to drive:

- away; away from the people, places, and things that no longer serve me
- forward; with a renewed sense of purpose and vision
- with intention; I will no longer allow other people's intentions, agendas, or poor behavior to drive me!

I'm going to drive! I am going to drive change! I'm going to drive by changing ME!

The Work:

1. What responses no longer serve me? To what new responses will I commit to drive the change I want to see?

2. What outdated perspectives am I maintaining? How can I evolve my thinking to ensure my success?

3. What position(s) have I taken that no longer hold? How can I reexamine my position and evolve?

With these new insights or awareness, what commitment will I make to myself or others?

_____

_____

_____

_____

_____

Chapter 37: What Are You Telling Your Clark Kent?

As I begin another new season, I am asking myself if I am dying under the weight of needing to be super:

- Superwoman?
- Supermom?
- Superstar employee?

I am asking myself how false narratives have driven me to exhaustion. Narratives like:

- Suck it up!
- Put on your big girl panties!
- You made this bed, now lie in it!
- Last hired, first fired!
- You don't have time to cry!
- You know we have to be better than everyone else!

In something akin to the dichotomy of Clark Kent and Superman, am I living a life of invisibility like Clark Kent while secretly trying to save or fix crises and situations because I believe I have to be a Superwoman?

This season, I release my need to fix and save everything and everyone. I choose to focus on the one person I can change, me! I will tell my Clark Kent:

- You don't have to work alone in silence!
- No one really leaps tall buildings in a single bound!
- You can't keep flying around looking for problems!

The Work:

1. How can I lead a more balanced life by partnering with others?

2. How can I empower others to solve their problems?

3. What practices or perspectives can I put in place to mitigate codependency, enmeshment, or people pleasing?

With these new insights or awareness, what commitment will I make to myself or others?

_____

_____

_____

_____

_____

Chapter 37: When

It's important to decide when. If we don't, we may not recognize that we have arrived.

While having breakfast with my dearest friend, she asked, "Tiffany, are you praying for a life you already have?"

It compelled me to consider:

- what I was praying for
- why I thought I didn't have it
- how I would know when I arrived
- why I was still waiting on my becoming

For many years, I had prayed to successfully raise my sons. As I reconsidered how I would know when this prayer was answered, I had to acknowledge that at 28 and 31 years old, I had raised them long ago. Moreover, I had conflated my successful raising with their successful being and all of the fears that come with raising children.

As a result, I had missed out on celebrating so many milestones, including opportunities to celebrate their independence, integrity, work ethic, and care for others.

I was so focused on praying through my fears, I had missed out on the opportunity to be grateful for their thriving.

Imagine that! Imagine you are still praying a prayer that has been answered a thousand times over! In so many areas of our lives we likely do because we have not taken the time to define our "when."

It is critical to define how you will know when you have arrived! If you don't, you may falsely perpetuate a narrative that robs you of your progress and peace.

As I carefully considered each of my prayers, I realized they were important prayers but prayers that were being incrementally answered. I was still praying to:

- be a leader
- have impact
- be a good wife, mother, and woman

Imagine the power of and need to shift my prayers to:

- Lord, help me to continue to be a leader of clear character, conviction and compassion!
- Lord, help me to continue to transform the systems that impact our daily lives in ways that ensure opportunity for all!
- Lord, continue to empower me to be the woman, wife and mother I need to be to deliver on the call you have on my life!

How might our perspective shift if we realized we had already arrived so it was time to chart a course for deeper impact or sustainability?

Today, I celebrate successfully raising two incredible men. I celebrate maintaining a marriage characterized by respect, unconditional love, fidelity, and peace. I celebrate being the kind of woman who genuinely wants the best for others, that will actively work to help others, that willingly gives to others, eschews gossip and divisiveness, and prays fervently for those I encounter.

This season, I give grace to myself and others, as I refine my discernment, prayers, and goals. Moreover, I acknowledge and give gratitude for graduating, being loving and accepting of others, hopeful, perseverant, accomplished, competent, and impactful.

The Work:

1. Have I determined what success is for me?

2. How will I know when I am successful?

3. How can I find and acknowledge success each day?

With these new insights or awareness, what commitment will I make to myself or others?

_____

_____

_____

_____

_____

Chapter 38: Old Habits Die Hard

Ever wonder why old habits die hard? Things like longing, fear, familiarity, hidden beliefs, and social pressure keep them alive and well! Despite what we might intellectually understand, our emotions can be a powerful draw.

If you have ever wavered in your resolve, you have the opportunity to ask why.

As you unpack the reasons why you have stayed longer than you should or went back and forth, chief among them can be drivers like belonging, uncertainty, and doubt.

Sometimes, we waver because we are unsure about what we need to do next.

Do you find yourself showing up to fights because you:

- don't know how to be at peace?
- feel obliged to participate?
- feel compelled to defend yourself?

Are you going back to relationships or staying in relationships because:

- they know you?
- you believe no one else will love you?
- something is better than nothing?

Is your resolve waning because:

- you have not seen immediate results?
- you are receiving social or peer pressure?
- you are uncertain whether your new approach will work or your new life will last?

As someone who has experienced several "firsts," had to be the first or only, or is trying something new by posting my thoughts, I can appreciate the fear of being judged, alone or in the minority.

This season, I ask you to join me in the brave work of trying, changing, and evolving!

This work requires you to risk being wrong, alone, different, and failing. The good news is that so do all of the behaviors you have been consistently doing as a result of history, trauma, fear, enmeshment, and people pleasing. The only difference is that you know you are tired of those results!

This season and every day forward, I am committing to:

- doing it afraid
- doing it alone
- doing it with opposition

Whatever my "it" is, I am committing to doing it no matter how scary or difficult it is because I deserve for someone to show up for me consistently, even if it's just me—and so do YOU!

The Work:

1. Am I maintaining habits that no longer serve me? If so, why? How can I develop new habits?

2. What steps can I take to ensure that I make progress? What commitment is needed to make progress? How will I monitor my actions to ensure consistent progress is made?

3. Have I relegated myself to unhealthy relationships, practices, or thinking? What shifts can I make to create the life I desire? How can I root out negative emotions like fear, doubt, shame, and guilt to make and sustain the change I desire? Where will I start?

With these new insights or awareness, what commitment will I make to myself or others?

_____

_____

_____

_____

_____

Chapter 39: Let the Light In

He said, "Let there be light!" and there was light. This powerful example grounds me in the knowledge that even in darkness, light can be declared. No matter how bleak or dark your situation, remember God declared, "Let there be light," and there was light.

Even when things feel largely shapeless or without direction, our Father has declared light. Whether it is a silver lining in our clouds or a rainbow at the end of a storm that has seemingly washed life away as we know it, God's precedence was to establish light in our dark world.

When the going gets tough, you may be tempted to go, tempted to:

- go it alone
- go around in circles; through circular reasoning and familiar patterns
- go into isolation, withdrawal or depression
- go away; till you discover that you take yourself everywhere you go, including your thinking, ways, and beliefs
- go along, even if it doesn't feel right, because everything else feels impossible
- go over it again and again; ruminate until you're apathetic

This season, I encourage you to go to the light! Each of the above-mentioned instances is an opportunity to let the light in. Whether it's the light or truth of the situation or our ability to find light at the end of our tunnel, if we will allow for light, we can illuminate our situations.

This illumination, when wielded, can bring us to new solutions, new opportunities, or resolution.

Consider the ways in which candles, beacons, light bulbs, and light posts work. When we allow light, even when the light may feel blinding or distant, it allows us to:

- find our way
- see the situation clearly
- negotiate a path forward

This season, I encourage you to seek ways to let light in. If you are in a dark situation, figuratively light a candle. Allow yourself to see where, with whom, or what you are contending. Falsely we may believe it's with someone. However, through my reflection journey, I am discovering it can be with:

- old beliefs and ways of being
- generational pathology
- overdue decision making
- other people's agendas, beliefs, and needs

Allow yourself to clearly see the battle, so you can clearly identify a winning strategy.

If you are feeling lost at sea, whether it's a sea of emotions or circumstances, figuratively look for a beacon. Look for something planted on where you want to go or able to guide you in the direction you need to be headed.

When I was awash with emotions or trauma, it was hard to see where I needed to go. Moreover, rough seas can have a dizzying effect. I liken it to being seasick and along for the ride. Sometimes, the ride was the voyage my family had taken for years. Other times it was the trips that happen when you are codependent, enmeshed, or just hurting.

Either way, it is critical to identify a beacon or a healthy point of reference. You don't have to wash ashore. You can dock in a safe place if you will allow yourself to be guided by a desire for peace, balance, or wholeness.

Lastly, if you have made the bold decision to chart a new path or enter new rooms, use the light post and/or turn on the light bulb. In new rooms, make sure you are not operating in the dark. This is not the time to wing it. Turn on the light and clearly identify the conditions so you can navigate accordingly. Similarly, if you are charting a new path for your family or yourself, look for the light posts along the way. Examples of light posts are mentors, coaches, sponsors, workshops, training, or any resources that can be leveraged to help you find your way.

So this season, let the light in!

The Work:

1. How can I illuminate my circumstances? How can I determine when I have resorted to negative coping like isolation, withdrawal, or projection? What will I do to interpret these counterproductive cycles in my life?

2. What am I doing to find my way? How am I working to see my situation clearly? What am I doing to find a path forward?

3. How am I working to ensure my beliefs, family history, choices, procrastination, or other people's agendas are not barriers to my progress? If they are, what will I do to mitigate these barriers? What commitment can I make today?

With these new insights or awareness, what commitment will I make to myself or others?

_____

_____

_____

_____

_____

Chapter 40: A New Birthday Wish

For many years, I made a wish and blew out candles on my birthday. As a child, my wishes were for tangible things like the newest toy. As I grew older, this cursory practice reflected situational considerations like wishes for love, peace, or prosperity.

This season, I reconsidered the practice of blowing out my light and hoping for something. After much reflection, I am deciding to institute a new practice. I am going to begin lighting or igniting my hopes.

Rather than lighting candles in remembrance of how many years have passed, I am committing to lighting a fire under my dreams. Whether it's a commitment to crossing something off my bucket list or adding a new skill to my repertoire, I'm going to live.

Next year, I will light a candle for the things I am doing this year to contribute to me living out my dreams. So far, I will light candles for:

- the book I am writing
- my new publisher
- my new website
- my first-ever advertisement

That's four candles and more to come. Come next year, I hope I have enough candles to burn the cake down. Minimally, I'm going to stop celebrating the passing of years and start celebrating the ways I am ensuring that I have a life well lived!

The Work:

1. What accomplishments or achievements can I light a candle for today?

2. By next year, how many candles would I like to light? What will I do to ensure there are candles to light next year?

3. How will I shift from counting my years to counting my living?

With these new insights or awareness, what commitment will I make to myself or others?

_____

_____

_____

_____

_____

Chapter 41: Actualizing Vision

Years ago, I realized that everyone who had achieved the things I wanted were putting their pants on one leg at a time like me. What I did not know was what they were doing after they had them on.

Sincerely desiring more for my life, I began revisiting what I did know. I harkened back to the lessons and adages I had heard along the way. Messages like "write the vision and make it plain," "a journey of a 1,000 miles begins with one step," and "you'll never finish if you don't start," became foundational.

With a commitment to this new foundation, I am putting each of these principles into practice through a strategic process.

First, I began with a vision board in recognition of the importance of "writing the vision and making it plain." Then I implemented a new step, an "accountability card."

My "accountability card" is my effort to begin taking steps towards my vision, with a clear sense of the target and what I need from myself and others. In the case of the vision that I have for my professional life, my "accountability card" includes commitments/steps that can be refined by using the SMART framework, goals that are: 1) specific, 2) measurable, 3) attainable, 4) realistic, and 5) time bound.

In order to ensure progress each week, I also implemented a "drive jar." It's a jar filled with the steps I take each week to accomplish my goals. It aids me in visualizing my progress while serving as a call to action. As my jar fills, I get the benefit of:

- tangibly seeing my progress in one place
- visually monitoring my progress each week
- being able to review my previous steps

This powerful exercise has allowed me to refine my process as I make progress.

One week, I reviewed the steps I had taken and I discovered that I was consistently taking steps in my comfort zone. Recognizing that I was taking a "low hanging fruit" approach to achieving my goals, I challenged myself to do something more difficult the next week. When I did, I got the gift knowing and noting that I could do hard things.

I call this a "compounding win" because I can leverage it as a reminder of my efficacy on my tough days.

As I continue this journey of yearlong reflection, I am heartened by the many gifts, reminders, learning, and unlearning along the way!

The Work:

1. What's on my accountability card? Am I holding myself accountable to it? As I review it, what am I discovering about my progress? Is further refinement needed?

2. How is my drive jar filling? Am I consistently taking steps to ensure progress? When are my greatest number of steps occurring? When are my least number of steps occurring? What differences am I observing in my progress? How can I capitalize on when I am most motivated? What steps can I take when I realize my progress is slowing?

3. How can I create more compounding wins in my life?

With these new insights or awareness, what commitment will I make to myself or others?

_____

_____

_____

_____

_____

Chapter 42: Living from the Possibilities

What would happen if we lived from the possibilities instead of perpetually managing for liability?

This weekend, I had a powerful conversation with one of my dearest friends. What began as a celebration of our resilience evolved into a deep recognition that I had anchored my experience in challenge. Rather than seeing the myriad opportunities I had experienced along the way, I had centered on my overcoming.

This centering meant I had experienced my journey as a series of challenges that I was consistently having to overcome.

After much reflection, I am now considering how my journey might feel differently if I saw life as a series of opportunities that I got to have no matter how bad things got.

What would happen if I embraced the belief that life is filled with possibilities, including some really great things?

What if I got to live and achieve as if there was a great life waiting to happen?

What if there wasn't:

- trouble lurking?
- a storm brewing?
- a monster under the bed or in the closet?
- an accident waiting to happen

What if there was just me, the possibilities, my gifts, my talents, an opportunity, and a chance?

This realization led me to the awareness that I had spent much of my life waiting for the other shoe to drop. My life has largely been a perpetual management of liability.

It also led me to the awareness that I had always had me, my talents, and my gifts. Moreover, after careful consideration and reflection, I realized I have had many opportunities and a real chance to do something impactful.

So today, I am challenging myself to live from the possibilities. Rather than walking on eggshells or holding my breath, I'm going to stand in the other truth of my experience.

My other truth is my life has been great in many ways. No matter what comes first, tribulation or triumph, I consistently experience wins and opportunities. Even my challenges can be understood as lessons wrapped in the gift of getting better.

With this reframing, I encourage you to consider how you have won.

I am considering how I have won and am embracing the possibility that success was never perfection or the absence of challenge. Rather, success is a process fueled by trial and error, practice and progress, as well as triumph and trial.

If you are having a difficult time seeing the possibilities or you are feeling downtrodden, I encourage you to begin living from the possibilities.

First, consider the possibility that there is another perspective, approach, or narrative you haven't considered, one that has you winning. Second, consider the treasure you have when you finally claim you—all of you, including your strengths, talents, gifts, and lived experience. Third, consider the power of the many tomorrows you have already had and the strength of surviving all of your yesterdays. Fourth, place each of your greatest challenges on individual pieces of paper. On the opposite side of the paper, write down the gifts or lessons that came from the challenge. Place these papers in a gift box.

The next time you are tempted to only acknowledge the challenge, open your gift box and remember what else you have gained.

Through this process, I came to realize that I gained tangible and intangible things that I wouldn't trade for anything. In my gift box are things like divorce, heartbreak, and grief. I also discovered that I had gained things like purpose, conviction, clarity, principle, and legacy from my challenge.

As you join me in challenging yourself to live from the possibilities, know that your gift box is filling even on your rough days!

The Work:

1. How can I begin to see my life through the lens of the possibilities and opportunities I have experienced? How might this shift my perspective? Practice? Goal setting? Vision? Actions?

2. What wins have I not recognized? What might these wins teach me about my prospects? How can I begin to embrace gratitude in recognition of all I have been given?

3. In what other ways can I live from the possibilities?

With these new insights or awareness, what commitment will I make to myself or others?

_____

_____

_____

_____

_____

Chapter 43: The Birthing Circle

This season, I was reminded of the stories of Sarah and Mary. Each gave birth in the most unconventional conditions, one seemingly birthing in shame and another birthing after most would say her season had passed.

Each birthing was in the most implausible conditions, but each birthing was in faith.

Imagine the lesson in this! Some of you may think, *It's too late.* Others may think, *But I didn't sign up for this.*

Either way, the moment demands that we must be of good cheer.

Whether you are waking from the hopelessness of believing your time has passed or you have been positioned for a birth for which you did not ask, there is a gift and purpose in your story.

You may have laughed out loud when seeing the glimmers of what could be birthed through you. You may be asking, how could this be visited upon me? Know that you are birthing in destiny.

As I consider what is being birthed in this season, I am thankful!

I'm thankful for the midwives in my life. I am grateful for the doula. I am thankful to be chosen. I am grateful it is never too late to birth what God has called me to deliver. I'm grateful that I don't have to know a man to do it. I'm thankful to have the kind of partner who trusts God and supports me fully through this birthing. I'm grateful that God gives me provision even when I'm in hiding from those who seek to terminate my birth. I'm thankful that God would shut my mouth before I would speak against my future.

This season, I'm just thankful!

This season, I work and walk in gratitude for the opportunity to give birth again.

The Work:

1. What am I being called to birth?

2. How can I see and remember that I am birthing even when I face challenges?

3. How can I refrain from speaking against the things I am birthing? How can I remember my purpose as I birth?

With these new insights or awareness, what commitment will I make to myself or others?

_____

_____

_____

_____

_____

Chapter 44: Go Higher

This season, I am committing to going higher. I am going higher in my valuing of self. I am redefining my femininity. I am allowing myself to be soft, loved, and supported.

For so long, being a woman and a mother meant I had to be prepared to save the world, my children, other people's children, communities, and possibly a nation, all while never letting anyone see me cry, complain, fail, or sweat.

While I acknowledged the weight of having to be a strong woman, I had not realized the callusing that ensues when there is no time to rest, heal, or hope. I had not considered the ways in which I had become hard-wired to ignore my needs.

Always "being ready" and vigilant was a badge of honor. I had not considered what it takes to be in a perpetual state of readiness. My definitions of mother, leader, friend, and family member left little room for the other ways I could be in relationship, partnership, or community with others. Often, connection meant coming to work, fight, or save. Rarely did I allow myself to ask, who was going to save me?

So this season, I am saving myself. I also encourage you to save yourself. Minimally, save yourself from:

- the unrelenting pressure of perfectionism
- the need to fix others
- the expectation of having all of the answers
- the responsibility for other people's emotions and actions
- carrying the weight of the world

This season, I encourage you to reconsider how you are defining things like femininity, masculinity, parenthood, partnership, or effectiveness.

If any of your definitions require you to do the work only others can do for themselves, deny your basic needs, enable rather than empower, be codependent, maintain a martyr complex, live in shame or denial, be absent from your life or live unconscious, you have an opportunity to go higher!

Some places to go higher include:

- boundaries
- downtime
- expectations
- sense of self-worth
- self-awareness
- peace
- balance
- hope

This season, I encourage you to go higher!

The Work:

1. Have I embraced going higher by maintaining appropriate boundaries, making time for self-care, and empowering others to solve their own problems?

2. Have I released my need to be perfect, save others, or be in control?

3. Am I defining my roles in ways that allow me to maintain balance, peace, and joy?

With these new insights or awareness, what commitment will I make to myself or others?

_____

_____

_____

_____

_____

Chapter 45: Redefining the Reset

This season, I am redefining my reset. I will no longer lament starting over.

This season, I acknowledge all that my reset can be. My reset can be:

- the precursor to a new beginning
- a lesson learned
- practice for my progress
- refinement
- trial and error
- experimentation
- preparation

It is my making. It is a predictable part of trying. It is an essential part of perfecting. It's the way I hone my craft.

It can be each of these things because I am finally acknowledging that something is gained, even in defeat.

It is the do-over I get when I risk trying again. It's my gift for not giving up. My reset is:

- a rebound
- a reprieve
- a second chance
- an opportunity for revelation

My reset can be a prologue in my book. It's the thing I do when I'm doing it again. It's my declaration that I can win.

So this season, I embrace my reset. I acknowledge that I am never just starting over again. I am trying again with the benefit of what I learned the last time.

The Work:

1. Am I defining my reset in ways that allow me to see opportunities?

2. Am I acknowledging what was gained last time?

3. Am I celebrating the gift of having another chance?

With these new insights or awareness, what commitment will I make to myself or others?

_____

_____

_____

_____

_____

Chapter 46: Carpe Diem

Ever wonder why someone might say, "Seize the day?"

It's because we must take our day by the horns! If we don't, our day can quickly become unruly. In a time when multitasking has become the norm and we are tethered to our phones, we can easily become distracted or overwhelmed if we don't identify our priorities and set boundaries.

Moreover, if you are prone to people-pleasing, your day can easily become one spent on someone else's emergency or needs.

This season, I am committing to "seizing the day" by:

- identifying and setting my priorities each day
- maintaining healthy boundaries
- making a daily to-do list that includes my needs and vision
- time-blocking and task-blocking to ensure the things that most matter are completed
- delegating and communicating to completion

Minimally, I am committing to these steps because experience has taught me:

- without daily priorities, I am subject to the whims, agendas, and priorities of others
- without healthy boundaries, I can become an enabler, subject to areas and roles of my life bleeding over into one another, or enmeshed in unhealthy dynamics
- without a to-do list that includes my vision for myself and my needs, I will find myself working at cross purposes and to exhaustion

- without time-blocking and task-blocking, I will rob myself of the satisfaction of completing identifiable tasks each day, and I may feel pulled in too many directions
- without delegation and communication to completion, I rob others of the opportunity to grow, learn, and shine.

I may also foster inner resentment and burnout because I am underutilizing others' gifts while encouraging burnout. Additionally, I may foster a pseudo sense of superiority by falling victim to false beliefs like only I can do it or it can't happen without me. Moreover, I rob myself of the vital communication essential to supporting myself and others, refinement, and course correction.

Accordingly, my work this season is not to lose sight of these vital leadership lessons and the strategies that have ensured my success!

The Work:

1. Am I consistently seizing my day by setting and maintaining my priorities? If not, why? How can I ensure that I am consistently addressing my priorities?

2. Does my to-do list consistently include action or steps to achieve my goals or vision?

3. Am I seizing the moments and opportunities when they occur? If not, why? What practices and perspectives can I put in place to ensure that I am seizing all of the great things my day holds?

With these new insights or awareness, what commitment will I make to myself or others?

_____

_____

_____

_____

_____

Chapter 47: And Once You've Been Freed

Sometimes change requires us to go cold turkey. There are some relationships, patterns, or situations that require us to stop, let go, or leave if we are to extract ourselves. When I finally had the courage to leave my marriage, unhealthy friendships, toxic workplaces, it required me to fully leave. It also required me to stop using the thinking, practices, and beliefs that had gotten me there. I could not date my ex-husband a little bit, or sometimes, and have a healthy new marriage. I could not maintain my codependence and find my independence or healthy interdependence. I could not promote and continue to play small. Recognizing that my wavering had me stuck, I say to you, "And when you are free, leave!"

Leave those old patterns of believing and being where they led you.

Embrace the new way of life with an enthusiasm that says you understand that you can't move forward by walking backwards.

There is no space for pretending a little. Your healing is one place where there is no middle ground. There is only being in the middle of the cycle again.

Just like it is unreasonable to believe that you can just drink a little, use a little, abuse a little, and be whole, it is unhealthy to make a living with a little abuse as the standard.

There is no little abuse. There is only the cycle. You are either in the beginning, middle, or end of the cycle. It's not just happening a little.

You may be tempted to believe that it looks or feels different, but those are only the old eyes, the blind eye, or the blinders obscuring the truth.

Progress can't be treated as a permit to go back. Save your new strength for the new life, the new opportunity, or the new season.

Don't give those old things another minute of your happiness, joy, or peace.

To risk the entanglement is to be entangled, entangled by the very thinking or behaviors that got you stuck, hurt, or broken.

If you must try out your new awareness, or apply your new skills, do it somewhere new.

Anything short of going somewhere else or doing something else is repeating the cycle again.

It's the old wine skin. Don't store your new wine there.

I am realizing that if I am to sustain my progress, it must be by "leaving behind those things that so easily beset me." Anything else leaves my healing to happenstance.

While I can do many things in moderation, moderation shouldn't be the standard for abuse. Self-abuse, accepting abuse, or living with abuse is abuse! The acceptance of abuse is fuel for the cycle.

I can't be a little good to myself and expect to be healthy and whole. Similarly, I can't accept a little abuse and call it a healthy situation, relationship, culture, or climate.

I can't engage a little with abuse and expect to be free.

Imagine leaving a plantation after decades of servitude. Could you really just clock in for a few shifts here and there?

Similarly, we must give ourselves the space, distance, time, and practice needed to fully live out our new freedom.

I acknowledge that this can be challenging, especially when you haven't physically, mentally, or emotionally left.

You may struggle with your new commitment while still navigating the same challenges, spaces, places, and people.

In these instances, our resolve must be to "stop." We can stop:

- participating in it
- accepting it
- telling ourselves it's impossible
- telling ourselves we are undeserving or unworthy
- wavering
- making excuses
- ignoring it
- pretending
- listening to the fears that keep us stuck, staying, or stagnant

This season, I commit to stopping the behaviors that no longer serve me. I also commit to moving:

- on!
- forward!
- up!

The Work:

1. What patterns, practices, or thinking must I relinquish to maintain my freedom, health, or peace?

2. What must I do to consistently maintain my progress in my previous areas of challenge?

3. What will I stop doing to have the life I desire?

With these new insights or awareness, what commitment will I make to myself or others?

_____

_____

_____

_____

_____

Chapter 48: Have You Met You?

Do you introduce everyone to your critic?

Do you carry your faults around instead of your resume?

Do you put up billboards of your greatest failures instead of skywriting your greatest wins?

If you are replying to every compliment with some backhanded comment about why you are not so great, it's time to meet you!

I encourage you to reintroduce yourself to you. When you do, be sure to do it as the person you are, not:

- the person you worried about becoming all of your life
- the you after your greatest failure
- as the statistics, misconceptions, and myths suggest

Rather, it is time to introduce yourself to the you that:

- survived
- overcame
- finished
- beat the odds

If you are uncertain who you are or your critic is winning out, take a moment to:

- update your resume
- write a new bio
- take a new headshot

These three steps should lead you to see who you are today, including:

- all your skill sets, competencies, and certifications

- the totality of your journey with its high points and your achievements
- who you are physically today
- what you readily bring to every relationship, table, and project
- why anyone would want to know you

This season, meet yourself!

The Work:

1. Am I evolving my perception of myself in real time?

2. What will I do to maintain a realistic perception of myself?

3. How can I take account of my talents, strengths, and knowledge in ways that empower me to achieve my goals?

With these new insights or awareness, what commitment will I make to myself or others?

_____

_____

_____

_____

_____

Chapter 49: Remember, It Is Not About the Gift Box. It's About the Gift in the Box!

Sometimes, we find ourselves in situations that seemingly appear troubling or daunting. We become distracted or despondent as we consider the prospects of our challenge. The challenge is just the box! Should we persevere, we will discover the real gift! The gift of resilience, the beauty of promise realized, new capacity, meaningful change, and breakthrough are the gifts we receive if we don't get discouraged by the packaging! Remember the gift today!

The Work:

1. What might I gain from this challenge? What practices, perspectives, or partnerships may be gained?

2. How can I be mindful of the opportunities this challenge holds?

3. What is the real gift in this challenge?

With these new insights or awareness, what commitment will I make to myself or others?

_____

_____

_____

_____

_____

Chapter 50: But Who's Showing Up to the "Living"?

My mom once said that for some people going to funerals is their favorite pastime. It made me consider all the ways we will show up for death, especially when we are stuck. Whether it's the death of a relationship, the death of our hopes, or the death of an era, we will REALLY show up!

We will lament, ruminate, and revisit our hurts, pains, and transgressions. We will replay dark times and recreate dark spaces.

It has me wondering what would happen if I showed up for my living in the same way. What if I paid homage to my hopes and dreams?

What if I recreated my successes?

What would happen if I revisited the possibilities and executed them?

Could my mourning become a new morning?

This season, I'm going to show up for my living!

The Work:

1. How am I dedicating my time and resources to things I want?

2. How am I embracing closure in the areas of life where resolution or healing is needed? What can I do to ensure my goals, passion, and peace are not consumed by remorse, regret, or envy?

3. What am I doing to ensure I am not living in the past? Am I maximizing my present by making progress, cultivating joy, and maintaining peace? Do I have a clear actionable vision for my future underway?

With these new insights or awareness, what commitment will I make to myself or others?

_____

_____

_____

_____

_____

Chapter 51: The Story of Almost

If you have been struggling with the things that almost happened in your life, you have an opportunity to reflect, reframe, release, and renew. If you are ruminating about what could have been, it is critical to first do the work of acceptance.

For me, this work has meant accepting that things are as they should be. It has also meant accepting that timing is divine. In some instances, it has required me to forgive myself for things I couldn't change at the time. As a result, I have forgiven myself for not knowing:

- better
- more
- different
- best

It has required me to forgive others, the process, and the systems. Particularly challenging were the instances where I questioned why this was my journey, lot, yoke, or cross. I have lamented immutable things like the plight of leading while being female, black, or misperceived.

Each of these things has required me to focus on realizing the deferred dream, raising lowered expectations, and turning exceptionalism on its head.

I've had to tell myself that my achievements were not a fluke, my opportunities were warranted, and my hopes were wholly feasible. More importantly, I have had to reflect, reframe, release, and renew:

- Reflect when I am consistently revisiting an event as failure instead of the many other things it could be, like a foreshadowing, a prerequisite, or practice

- Reframe the event in ways that empower me to move forward, extract the lesson, deepen my skills, clarify my vision, or refine my process
- Release the shame, fear, doubt, guilt, or foreboding that ensues when you believe you missed an opportunity, made the wrong decision, or took the wrong turn
- Renew my focus, effort, commitment, intention, or the strategies that worked for me

Most importantly, it requires me to resist the "story of almost," a story about how I almost had the life I wanted.

If you are still living, you have an opportunity to make it real! Of all of the things you may choose to accept, don't accept the "story of almost."

The Work:

1. Have I forgiven myself?

2. What is it to find acceptance? Where can I embrace acceptance to move forward in my life goals? How can I ensure that I only accept the things that allow me to maintain my well-being?

3. What can I do to ensure that I don't settle for "almost" achieving my goals and vision?

With these new insights or awareness, what commitment will I make to myself or others?

_____

_____

_____

_____

Chapter 52: Picking Up Tabs

We must be mindful of where and how often we pick up the tab—the emotional tab.

If we are not careful to maintain boundaries, honor our needs, trust our intuition, and use our voices, we may find ourselves bearing the emotional weight of other people's hurts, choices, and challenges.

In something akin to picking up the tab at a bar, we may find ourselves taking responsibility for other people's actions or acting according to other people's expectations.

With a yearlong commitment to reflection underway, this weekend, I am unpacking the places, people, and issues that compel me.

If there are areas, relationships, or issues in your life where you consistently feel compelled to fight, defend, or prove, you have an opportunity to ask why.

After much reflection, I am discovering that some of these battles are the result of toxic narratives. Chief among them are the narratives of:

- the strong black woman
- the angry black woman
- working twice as hard
- saving the world, my community, or others
- being humble
- being forgiving
- being magical

The strong black woman narrative leaves me little space to be tired, hurt, or sad. The angry black woman narrative leaves me overly polite, diplomatic, and silenced in some instances. The narrative that I must work twice as hard or be twice as good to have parity has me overworked and always second-guessing myself.

The belief that I must save my community has me responding to a cause or problem every week. The narrative that I must be humble has me minimizing my strengths, gifts, and potential. The narrative that I must be forgiving has me ignoring bad behavior, managing other people's fragility, and making excuses for grown people. The narrative of black girl magic has me striving to appear magical on my ordinary days.

The totality of these things has me living up to or down to something every day while I fight against exceptionalism.

I am also seeing the tabs I pick up as a result of generational pathology, patriarchy, and trauma. I am carrying the generational trauma of people who predate my existence. I am carrying my grandmother's pain and my mother's hurts. Daily, I navigate any number of systemic isms. Then, there is the weight of what happened to me.

So this season, I am mindful that it's okay to pick up a tab or two. With this awareness, I am grounded by activism and proud of my advocacy in the rooms where I am the "first" or "only."

I am also mindful that no one can sustain picking up the tab all of the time. With this acknowledgment, I have begun choosing my battles. Today, I am also mindful that I get to choose. With this new freedom, I am also choosing where and when I will pick up the tab.

The Work:

1. Are there areas in my life where I am consistently compelled to fight, defend, or prove myself? If so, why?

2. Am I allowing external narratives like stereotypes to drive my decision-making?

3. How can I reclaim my balance by identifying and focusing on my priorities?

With these new insights or awareness, what commitment will I make to myself or others?

_____

_____

_____

_____

_____

Chapter 53: Halfway There!

Today is an incredible day! It's the official signal of the halfway point! For some, it's the beginning of a new fiscal year. Either way, it is a great time to celebrate, concentrate, and reinvigorate if needed.

If you are operating from a calendar year, it is a great time to celebrate all that you have accomplished thus far. With a commitment to living a more conscious life, I encourage you to:

1. Revisit your New Year's resolutions to celebrate the ways you are honoring those commitments to transformation.

2. Review all that you have achieved so far, including any incremental progress and gains in each area of your life: career, education, family, relationships, physical health, mental health, finances, and other areas.

3. Celebrate that you are still here no matter what the first half of the year has thrown your way.

4. Celebrate the ways you have contributed to a brighter future for your family, the community, your relationships, and yourself. This list includes things like voting, advocacy, and volunteerism.

I am personally celebrating a half-year of new initiatives and all of the things that go into a successful year, including collaboration and new partnerships, investment in myself and others, improved communication, the successful completion of the annual operations plan, the successful administration of several grants, and the chance to do more!

As I reviewed my "Drive Jar," a jar of Post-its highlighting the steps I take towards my goals each week, there were 30-plus items in the jar. It included things like launching a blog, establishing a website, and doing my first advertisement. Suffice it to say, there is a great personal celebration underway!

This is also a great time to concentrate! Consider concentrating your efforts on the areas where more progress is needed and the areas close to completion. I like the balance of completing goals that can be achieved with a short-term focus and the notion of playing the "long game."

Accordingly, I use this time of year to identify a mix of goals that can be completed in the next quarter and one or more goals that are slated for completion in the next 48 months. This process ensures that I will have wins by the end of the year with demonstrable progress towards my long-term goals.

To aid in building this list, review your resolutions, work plan, the organization's operations and strategic plans, your savings and portfolio, and your health goals. Also, consider establishing a family plan for review. Each of these plans or goals is an opportunity to concentrate on making tangible progress.

Lastly, I encourage you to reinvigorate! If your focus, vision, or efforts have fallen by the wayside, reinvigorate by refocusing, renewing, reestablishing, and reprioritizing!

Refocus on the vision you have for yourself, your why, and the legacy you hope to leave.

Renew your efforts—go back to the gym, meal planning, the basics, or whatever foundational skills are needed to achieve your goals.

Reestablish the habits, support, and thinking you leveraged when you were making progress. This could include reconnecting with your support group and/or accountability partner. It could entail returning to mediation, yoga, or maintaining a daily to-do list. It may also mean being more conscious of your decision-making and patterns. It is critical to ensure that the boundaries, balances, and balls you maintain serve you!

Finally, reprioritize YOU—your needs, your desires, and your vision. You won't get your first things if they are consistently at the bottom of the list or out of sight and out of mind. Use this halfway point to make it the rest of the way!

Now that we are halfway there, let's make it the rest of the way together!

The Work:

1. On what goals or areas of my life should I refocus? Where have I lost sight of my vision? What have I forgotten? What commitments or priorities would benefit from renewed focus?

2. Where in my life is renewal needed? In what areas or practices has my commitment waned? What do I need to begin doing again?

3. What can I reestablish to further my goals? Align my vision? Ensure completion?

With these new insights or awareness, what commitment will I make to myself or others?

_____

_____

_____

_____

_____

Chapter 54: I'm Going on Maternity Leave!

This season, I had a profound conversation with some incredible leaders. While visioning together, someone remarked, "I'm going on maternity leave so I can birth self-hope!"

This likening to birth and the need for maternity leave moved me.

During my lifetime, I have birthed and watched others' births.

Rarely was the allotted time taken to heal, bond, or define the new pace needed for the new role.

We cite the need to work or financial challenges as the reason for our early return.

In other instances, we exhaust leave and lament the transition wasn't sufficiently supported.

Either way, we must acknowledge that the process of birthing, whether life or promise, places a demand on the laborer.

Metaphorically, there is the carrying that happens until birth can occur. It is tantamount to the stewardship that must occur when we hope to deliver change.

Parallels can be drawn between crowning, the period before arrival, where you must bear down, but the baby is certain to come.

In our work, we often must push and bear hardest when we are closest to realizing the vision.

There are also the parallels that can be drawn between the last trimester. It is the most uncomfortable period, in some respects. It is the time of greatest swelling. The baby drops in preparation for labor. You may even experience Braxton Hicks contractions, false labor.

In so many respects, the journey of systemic change, transformation, and realizing vision requires us to carry, labor, and crown before we deliver in ways akin to the birthing process.

Not until this moment had I considered that rest is needed in the same ways maternity leave is needed after giving birth.

Because I was running from poverty, I never stopped to rest after birthing.

In one eleven-year period, I completed four degrees, divorced, moved out of state, began a consulting firm, wrote 16 publications, bought a home, became a single parent, and cried because I didn't feel I was good enough.

In a subsequent six-year period, I joined a sorority and two professional women's organizations, bought another home, remarried, held roles as COO, CEO, and executive director, and was even a member of a governor's cabinet, but I still struggled with self-doubt.

I am also acknowledging that I have been laboring, or in labor for change, for over a decade, in many of the systems that impact my community. Consider the labor and delivery associated with:

- education reform
- juvenile justice reform
- healthcare reform
- justice reform and reentry

In each of these areas, I serve on a commission or board in hopes of realizing change.

I now wonder how my experience of myself and these efforts might feel differently if I made time for rest or leave.

If your journey is anything like mine, you are likely in some stage of pregnancy or birthing. Wherever you are in the process, don't forget to schedule "maternity leave."

The Work:

1. How can I begin acknowledging and attending to the rest needed to make and sustain change?

2. What commitment can I make to begin fostering the rest needed to sustain the work?

3. What is my self-care plan for ensuring ongoing consistent rest?

With these new insights or awareness, what commitment will I make to myself or others?

_____

_____

_____

_____

_____

Chapter 55: Clear

This season, I'm getting clear!

I am going to get clear about myself! While I have long had a sense of purpose, I have not always had a clear sense of what makes me happy or even who I am when I am not trying to be who society says I need to be.

It's like having a clear "why" but a shifting sense of "who" or "what." While I expect my "how" to evolve as time and climate shift, I am exploring what it is to be true to myself.

This season, I am asking, "What would Tiffany do?"

What would I do if I was not beholden to anyone else's expectations, hurts, agendas, problems, or perspectives? Who am I in the absence of fixing, problem-solving, or performing—performing all of the duties associated with the hats I wear?

Ultimately, my ability to be at peace is having a clear standard for living with myself.

If I don't know who I am, I can't answer the question, "Am I okay with me at the end of the day?"

I think that part of my internal conflict is the way in which the world requires me to shift my "how" in ways that are inconsistent with my "who." The pretense of being okay with the ways others are showing up or acting can be debilitating.

You may think silence is solace, but it isn't when it feels like tacit approval.

I am most troubled in those moments when I am asking myself:

- "Are you really going to let that pass?"

- "Are you okay with that?"
- "Are you really not going to say anything?"
- "Are you really not going to do anything?"

I am not a bystander.

What do you do when climate, culture, and shifting societal norms are asking you to idly stand by and do nothing or say nothing?

I never wanted to be a bystander in my life, and I don't want to be a bystander to injustice. In my mind, there is no innocent bystander, when you watch others be persecuted and expect the transgression not to be visited upon you.

In my dispassion, I hear the echoes of my early years:

- "Our lives begin to end the day we become silent about the things that matter."
- "Injustice anywhere is a threat to justice everywhere."
- "A man who stands for nothing will fall for anything."

I am reminded that my mother often says, "Tiffany, you can be pitiful or powerful, but you can't be both."

What is the balance to strike when you are tired of fixing but you can't stand idly by?

I think the list of things I am clear about are:

- Everyone needs grace.
- Everyone should have peace.
- Dignity, humanity, worth, and well-being shouldn't be contingent on your zip code, bank account, or station in life.

What I am unclear about is what to do when these things aren't the case.

Just being angry about it isn't enough. Moreover, being angry while being a black woman isn't allowed. Hence, my dilemma. What do I do if my "who" isn't allowed?

I think my work in this season is to figure out what the standard is for me. Am I willing to compromise who I am for the sake of making progress towards my why?

In many respects, this is the nature of the code-switching required each day. In order to be gainfully employed, I am required to only bring parts of myself to the work.

Similarly, in order to navigate shifting political winds, we are required to consciously calculate what we will say or do.

What do you do when it's your existence or rights at stake?

While I'm not clear about the answer, I am clear about my commitment to finding an answer.

I'm committed to this journey of discovery!

The Work:

1. How can I maintain authenticity in the face of oppression, subjugation, and persecution? How can I contribute to social change while maintaining psychological safety? What action can be taken to ensure progress and balance coexist?

2. Have I allowed exhaustion to relegate me to being a bystander? If so, how can I renew my focus? How can I engage in sustainable ways?

3. What is it to be true to myself? How am I honoring my needs while contributing to change? What will I do to maintain balance?

With these new insights or awareness, what commitment will I make to myself or others?

_____

_____

_____

_____

_____

Chapter 56: Maybe You Are Being Called to Learn?

Today, I am pondering the turbulence I've experienced over the course of my journey. I am considering the possibility that maybe those experiences were designed for me to learn. Maybe the opposition or resistance is about me developing:

- a new perspective
- a new skill
- a new ally
- a stronger case
- new ground

Many times, the resistance has felt like a deliberate effort to thwart my progress. Today, I am considering why God allowed it. Maybe the thing that felt like my "breaking" was really my "making."

I am asking, "Is there a possibility that the thing that needs to change is me?" even if it's just:

- knowing when to choose my battles
- holding space for other people, ideas, and opportunities
- distinguishing between seasons
- recognizing it's rarely about me, but my journey and learning are about me

This season, I am open to just learning, even if it's just learning what's not for me!

This Work:

1. Are there lessons in this experience that I am neglecting?

2. Are there hidden wins in this experience?

3. Are there alternative ways of viewing resistance, such as viewing it as learning, practice, or protection?

With these new insights or awareness, what commitment will I make to myself or others?

_____

_____

_____

_____

_____

Chapter 57: But Are You Pleased?

As I unpack people pleasing, I am realizing I'm not pleased. I'm not pleased with the ways that it:

- robs me of my personhood
- runs counter to my self-care
- denies my needs
- fosters resentment
- situates others as the authority on my worth

Most troubling is the way it requires me to be a contortionist, chameleon, and an afterthought.

It's the way it has me responding to moving targets, spoken and unspoken expectations, and whims.

It's the way that people-pleasing subtly communicates that I can and should be all things to all people, in all places, and whatever is needed.

It's the way that people pleasing doesn't care that:

- it's not my issue
- it's someone else's problem
- it's enabling
- it disempowers
- it's not sustainable

I am not pleased with people pleasing because it leaves me displeased with myself, others, and situations.

It's the way people pleasing causes me to ask myself:

- Why won't I stand up for myself?
- Why did I let them dump that on me again?
- Where is my voice and my needs in all of this?

It's the way I am pleased when they say, "We couldn't have done it without you," and I smile.

It's the way I forget that I have children, a husband, and needs, too, as they leave me holding the bag, catching the hot potato, and accepting excuses.

I think my work this season is to figure out how pleasing people serves me, stop it, and begin maintaining healthy boundaries. Then, I will be pleased!

The Work:

1. How does people pleasing serve me? What need is it meeting? How can I address the need so I can begin maintaining healthy boundaries and relationships?

2. When I am neglecting my needs and priorities to people please, how can I identify what is occurring and counteract the behavior?

3. What new practice or perspective will I adopt to mitigate my people-pleasing?

With these new insights or awareness, what commitment will I make to myself or others?

_____

_____

_____

_____

_____

Chapter 58: Don't Get Distracted

There is a divine unfolding underway. Each of us has a purpose, and in accordance with this purpose, there is a plan unfolding.

We can be tempted to believe that everything is happenstance. Only in hindsight, or in the rearview mirror of our lives, can we see the intricate weaving of our journey. That's why it is important to not get distracted.

Lest we tame our expectations or beliefs about how things could have been or our "shoulds," we may miss the opportunity to celebrate and affirm the journey underway.

For years, I lamented the pace of things and grieved all of the things I thought I missed along the way. I mourned not the things that passed but rather the things I thought must have passed because of what I chose, or did, or did not do.

I lost sight of all the things that happened that were not in my wildest dreams but were wildly amazing! I did not take account of all the gifts and unanticipated new beginnings along the way.

Had I had my way or my fears, there would have been no redemption or surprises. So today, I am reminding myself to not get distracted.

I am remembering to lean into the turn, embrace the curve, and be grateful for the reroute. I am remembering that the purpose of the detour is to ensure our safety and our arrival.

I am celebrating all of the things I never received, the doors that never opened, and the ones that did to my amazement. I am relaxing in the knowledge that I don't have all of the knowledge, but I do have things like hope, faith, and trust.

As I check my rearview mirror today, I can see a divine overcoming that is still unfolding. In gratitude, I celebrate becoming a doctor, raising successful sons, becoming a homeowner, being happily married—being above the average in so many regards.

This gratitude is not to negate the very real challenges we face each day but rather an acknowledgment of a scripture that has been foundational for me:

"No weapon that is formed against thee shall prosper; and every tongue that shall rise against thee in judgment thou shalt condemn. This is the heritage of the servants of the LORD, and their righteousness is of me, saith the LORD." Isaiah 54:17 KJV

The statistics suggest I shouldn't or couldn't be all that I am—yet I AM!

With this awareness, I powerfully reframe the doubts, the stares, and the admonition. I resist distraction.

I embrace the journey as it is.

The Work:

1. In what ways can I demonstrate my commitment to embracing the journey?

2. How can I consistently remember that there is a divine plan unfolding, one that accounts for everything that has occurred?

3. How can I continue to inhabit a space of gratitude?

With these new insights or awareness, what commitment will I make to myself or others?

_____

_____

_____

_____

_____

As I consider the insights and awareness gleaned from this season, what commitments to myself or others am I measuring, monitoring, and adjusting as needed, to ensure my success?

_____

_____

_____

_____

_____

_____

_____

_____

_____

_____

_____

_____

_____

_____

_____

_____

_____

_____

Summer

My summer season was a very painful time. Daily I was being impacted by gossip, toxicity, and a social competition for which I had never signed up. Initially I did not realize the ways in which childhood bullying, my history of being in relationship with narcissists, and my need for belonging, were converging to leave me feeling powerless. In time, I would realize the deleterious effects of the othering that occurs in all of our lives. It was this othering that would become the most powerful lesson of my season.

The Obstacles from Othering

I have had to live with "othering" all my life. Othering is the process of socially constructing difference to facilitate dominance. Before this season, I only understood othering through the lens of the isms I grapple with each day. I now realize other things about othering like:

- Othering begats othering
- Sometimes we other ourselves
- Some people do not know who they are if they are not othering you

Moreover, othering is a divisive strategy designed to foster an us versus them mentality where individuals fight to be part of the in crowd by pushing others out. It is facilitated through practices like microaggressions, stereotypes and prejudice so othering can become self perpetuating. Its subjects go from being hated to self-hatred.

Othering is an effort to gain and maintain power. Its results are exclusion, lowered aspirations and low expectations, pigeonholing, and the deferral of dreams. Grounded in scarcity, inferiority and fear, othering colors the truth. It paints a picture that enacts dehumanization, xenophobia, nationalism, segregation, caste-like systems, and a competition where few can win.

Now I understand othering's intent, its purpose, its role, its strategy and the ways in which it's about:

- Someone else's fear
- Someone else's inadequacy
- Someone else's weak ego
- Someone else's weak identity
- SOMEONE ELSE

As a result of this new awareness, I am no longer trying to be anything or anyone other than who I am. I now see their gossip as a weak attempt to feel better about themselves, mitigate their feelings of inadequacy, and maintain a power that feels fleeting. It also compels me to do the work of addressing my own feelings of inadequacy, powerlessness, and fear. As I do, I am able to extend grace in spite of their bad intentions, bad behavior, and faulty thinking.

As you read the reflections that follow, I hope you will consider how we may free ourselves and free each other by cultivating wholeness.

Chapter 59: My Rose-Colored Glasses Are Red!

I am realizing that my rose-colored glasses are actually red.

Rather than seeing the world through an optimistic, upbeat, rosy lens, I've been seeing it through the code-switching required in most spaces, the microaggressions I manage daily, and the stereotypes that ensnare my hopes and my dreams.

My lens is warped by the fear of being perceived as an angry Black woman. It's almost like a pair of shades whereby I never see the full light of the possibilities for me.

I'm seeing everything but in the slightly dimmer light of:

- other people's expectations
- unrealized aspirations
- the residue of generational trauma

Some days, the weight of "being" is so heavy my rose-colored glasses feel like cataracts by the time I'm done processing "being":

- a woman
- Black
- a mother
- an employee
- an "other"

With this awareness, I now have the gift of processing what's going on when I'm seeing "red."

Maybe the red is the flag I am wired to see to know when to code switch.

Maybe it's the hopelessness I feel when I remember no amount of education, skill, hard work, or effort has allowed me to avoid being misunderstood, misused, or accused.

Maybe it's the sadness I feel when all I want to do is just "be," but I'm being gaslit, told:

- "That's not what happened!"
- "That's not what's happening!"
- "That's not what's going to happen."
- "That doesn't happen."
- "That did not happen!"

My glasses are red because it HAPPENS! It's HAPPENING!

With this new awareness, I'm going to work on cleaning my glasses. I might even take them off from time to time so I can see the world as it is.

Maybe that's the work for me. Maybe the work is not to see the world as it could or should be but rather to see it as it is and make peace with it.

This season, I will do some work. I will develop a new, more effective kind of peace, a peace rooted in a vision of MY making.

The Work:

1. What isms are at play in my environment? Dualism? Classism? Sexism? Racism? Ageism? Capitalism? Other isms? How can I unpack the isms that occur in my environment and package them in ways that enable me to maintain psychological, emotional, physical, and financial safety?

2. What immediate, mid-term, and long-term strategies can I employ to mitigate the impact of isms individually, organizationally, systemically, or globally? How can I prioritize the strategies to

ensure my psychological safety, a healthy organizational culture, a functional family system, a healthy community, or a just nation?

3. How might interpersonal, transgenerational, or tertiary trauma inform my experience? Am I able to define when trauma is compounding? If so, have I identified successful strategies for unpacking "layered" traumatization?

With these new insights or awareness, what commitment will I make to myself or others?

_____

_____

_____

_____

_____

Chapter 60: The Price of Invisibility

Invisibility costs! It's the way you don't see opportunities for others while they are holding on to hope.

It's the hole where the pigeon dropped their aspirations.

It's different from the black ball. It's as if they are of no consequence.

This lack of consequence, this purported insignificance, has a cost.

The world misses out on their gifts, and they miss out on:

- realizing their potential
- bits and parts of their future
- their firsts

This invisibility threatens to upend their destiny. It is the thing that makes meritocracy a myth.

It's the thing that takes the straps out of their boots.

It's the thing that keeps the field where they play uneven.

It puts the "e" on the cast in the middle of their award-worthy performance.

It heckles them. It says things like:

- "Don't nobody care about you!"
- "Ain't nobody talking to you!"
- "Ain't nobody looking for you!"

Sometimes it even yells, "You ain't nobody!"

It's the way it has both of us on the spot, even if it's just in a blind spot.

It's the way we can't see them at all.

We can't see their pain, their potential, their strengths, or our opposition.

In the rare instances when we do see them, we imbue them with our fears and the darkest things.

This invisibility costs. As I take account, I realize it is a toll that is compounding.

It's the way that I feel unseen, so I don't expect to be seen.

It's the way no one asks me, so I stop asking.

It's the way no one hears me, so I become silent.

Most profound is the way invisibility is compounded by the mask and the bushel.

The mask I wear obscures me. The bushel I lie beneath dims me.

You see my assimilation, my code switch, and all those mainstream devices, but you do not see me.

Behind the wig, behind the wares, is this woman.

Resilient, brilliant, and competent is this woman.

Not always strong, not angry, not just resilient, is a woman in this invisibility waiting to be seen.

This year, I commit to seeing myself and seeing others in all their complexity, but most importantly, their humanity.

This season, I will take off the mask and begin this new journey by seeing me!

The Work:

1. Why am I feeling unseen? What situational, systemic, and individual factors are at play? How can I address these factors for myself and others?

2. What is invisibility currently costing me in time, health, opportunity, relationships, or other areas? How can I mitigate this impact?

3. Have I allowed myself to become complicit in my invisibility or the invisibility of others? If so, how? What immediate, mid-term, and long-term strategies will I undertake to mitigate this complicity?

With these new insights or awareness, what commitment will I make to myself or others?

_____

_____

_____

_____

_____

Chapter 61: It's Crazy!

You are crazed!

It's the way you spin up and wind down to create a crisis so you can save.

It's the way you want to be hope, but everyone around feels hopeless, hopeless about you ever-changing your ways.

It's the way you want to save but won't save yourself. Get therapy, get medication, get help, get away!

Did you know that it's crazy to tell me one thing, do another, and try to convince me I'm not seeing what I am seeing?

What's crazy is that we have not left you, held you accountable, or called you out, because you do it so frequently.

Some of us have accepted it. We say things like:

- "That's just them."
- "That's just the way it is."
- "I'm just going to focus on what I'm doing."

We pretend with you! We pretend we are not seeing what we are seeing, hearing what we are hearing, or feeling what we are feeling.

We pretend until we are no longer pretending.

Your crazy making and craziness are so insidious that they spread. We begin to think that we are crazy. We say things like, "Maybe there's another way to see it" until we don't see it at all.

We say maybe there's another way to interpret what you are saying until we stop saying anything.

We say maybe you didn't mean that until we can't decipher your intentions, the consistent source of the confusion, and the way you make things crazed around you.

I think the work for me is to understand that I can't change you. I can't protect you. I can't protect those around you. But I must protect myself.

I must stay firmly rooted in my knowing.

Most importantly, I must not lose sight of my ability to choose, to choose safety and peace.

The Work:

1. How can I maintain clarity, boundaries, and peace in these situations?

2. Why am I remaining in this situation? What do I hope to gain by staying? When will I choose to leave?

3. How is my response contributing to this challenge? What aspects of this challenge should I own? What is an appropriate response to this challenge? How can and will I appropriately address this challenge?

With these new insights or awareness, what commitment will I make to myself or others?

_____

_____

_____

_____

_____

Chapter 62: Hey, What Are You Doing with the Truth?

I am astounded by what people will do with the truth. I shouldn't be, especially when I acknowledge how trauma, mental illness, agendas, aims, and other factors can drive people to do strange things with the truth.

I have seen people take the truth and:

- distort it
- deny it
- wash it
- twist it
- manipulate it
- run from it
- hide it

Like an ostrich with its head in the sand, I have even seen myself avoid it.

I am finding that it is critical to identify and address when something is happening with the truth. If I'm not careful to identify when something is happening to the truth, I can become emotionally hijacked, gaslit, manipulated, or stagnant. I may even become despondent or apathetic.

I think part of my work this season is to consistently identify when something is happening with the truth and be clear about what I need to do about it.

Some critical questions, I am asking myself are:

- Why are they distorting, hiding, or manipulating the truth?
- How are they or I served by my response?

- How can I be an accountability partner in this situation, for myself or others?
- How do I remain grounded in truth as the manipulation and gaslighting ensue?
- What boundaries are needed to address what is happening with the truth?

This approach and inquiry is a significant shift for me. Before I began acknowledging the ways in which agendas, aims, or traumas informed what people did with the truth, I often led from a place of grace only. I found myself making excuses and saying things like:

- Maybe they are misunderstood?
- They are doing the best they can.
- Maybe it was an accident?
- They heard me this time so next time will be different.

With a commitment to seeing the truth of the matter, I am now acknowledging other possibilities:

- They intended what they did.
- This exchange is not about the truth. It is about a particular aim or agenda.
- This is their way of being.
- The goal isn't clarity.

In time, I hope to develop a new approach. In doing so, I believe I can be at peace with:

- Agreeing to disagree
- Accepting people as they are, even when they are trying to manipulate me
- Choosing my battles because it's not a "battle of perceptions"
- The fact that many people lie, even if it's just to themselves.

With this new awareness, I'm going to do the work of maintaining my peace, choosing my battles, and standing in my truth, even in the face of gaslighting and manipulation.

If I am doing anything other than embracing truth and standing by it, I am going to shift!

The Work:

1. In instances where distortion is the result of fear or judgment, how can I foster or support the conditions needed for transparency? How might I positively contribute to the psychological safety needed for authenticity?

2. When there is a discrepancy, how can I support others to maintain their truth while honoring my truth? Am I allowing for varying perspectives, philosophies, or other factors that may be informing another individual's sense of the truth?

3. If a truth is in question, do I need to determine its accuracy? How do I empower myself to maintain my authenticity and psychological safety while allowing for differing truths?

With these new insights or awareness, what commitment will I make to myself or others?

_____

_____

_____

_____

_____

Chapter 63: Where I Come From...!

I recently heard myself say. "Where I come from..."

I think it was an attempt to explain what felt like some inherent differences in:

- perspectives
- rules of engagement
- beliefs
- philosophies

Whatever it was, I left feeling misunderstood, gaslit, and vulnerable.

If all of the above-mentioned things informed the task at hand, no wonder tasks together feel challenging at times.

I fundamentally believe that it is not because we want it to be a challenge, but rather, everything on the above mentioned list is up for debate!

Accordingly, I think some of my work this season is to get clear about where I do come from.

It may be my only hope to understand where they are coming from in these interactions.

Maybe just recognizing that we each come from our experience and that there's no way that could be the same thing will help.

Maybe the work is recognizing that we don't have to share the same perspective, philosophy, rules of engagement, or beliefs to agree on an approach and commit to an outcome.

Maybe the work is about letting go of how I feel when the rules of engagement conflict with my values.

In the moments when my inner voice is saying, *I would never*:

- *say that to someone.*
- *do that to someone.*
- *treat them like that.*

I have an opportunity to say, "You would not because you are not them! You are just coming from where you come from, and they are just coming from where they come from."

I'm still not sure how we will come together, but I am exploring whether it's possible to come together with our differences in perspective, rules, and beliefs by just agreeing on the result.

As I ponder this prospect, I am saying to myself that it must be or become possible because it's the only way we are going to solve poverty, racism, hunger, or any other social issue together.

I think the work I can do right now is to explore where I come from and how these interactions leave me feeling unseen, unheard, and disrespected.

It's in their "All you have to do is" that the negative feelings come up.

My inner voice cries, "What do you know about what I have to do? Have you considered how debilitating it is to have to make everything your good idea, even my very existence here in this place, in this country?

"Have you considered the psychological tax I pay every day by code-switching, contorting, and pretending to need to be saved so you feel positive about your ability to make a difference?

"Have you considered the weight of constantly choosing between this tax and going back to the poverty tax?"

As I write, I realize there is more to unpack, but I can start with one thing.

This season, I will work to come from a place of peace, grace, and acceptance. I will embrace the serenity of changing what I can, considering acceptance for what I can't, and consistently identifying the difference.

The Work:

1. In conflict, am I able to discern when a difference of opinion, philosophy, approach, or priority is occurring? If so, how do I work to address these differences?

2. When conflict is the result of coercive practices such as manipulation, deception, or gaslighting, am I able to discern these intentions? If so, do I have a strategy for maintaining psychological safety?

3. How is where I come from informing my interactions with others? Are there conflicting norms at play? Is there unaddressed trauma at play? How might I view these exchanges if I accounted for these factors?

With these new insights or awareness, what commitment will I make to myself or others?

_____

_____

_____

_____

_____

Chapter 64: I'm Tired of Being Co*nscious!

Recently someone suggested that working within systems to foster change is selling out. As someone serving on several boards and commissions to effect change, this comment was an affront. Moreover, it compelled me to consider some of the criticism I have heard over the years regarding nonviolent protest and code-switching.

As someone navigating advocacy, in my skin, in this culture, there are ways in which managing the subtle backdrop of not being perceived as the "angry Black woman" can be debilitating. When you layer this management with the need to code switch, it can be overwhelming. Coupling these expectations with not being perceived as black enough, or vocal enough, activism can be demoralizing.

After spending a day carefully building consensus for investments in an issue disproportionately impacting young unemployed Black males, I overheard someone say, "She's always using big words. It doesn't take all that."

I lamented this comment. As a mother of two young men, an African American woman, uniquely positioned to see the inequities that occur in systems each day, I feel it takes much more than just having a message. My work requires me to actively consider the message, messenger, receiver, and subtle dimensions like tone and tenor. Moreover, the fact that my passion is sometimes misconstrued as anger adds another dimension to the task of advocacy.

However, most troubling was that this conversation was transpiring between two Black women. It reminded me that I was tired because sometimes I find myself fighting with the people for which I am fighting–figuratively fighting to live up to their expectations while fighting systems to live up to the charge of equality and equity.

Moreover, I was disheartened to be criticized for my diction and word choice by women who looked like me.

Here's my reflection from the evening of this exchange:

I Am Tired of Being Coonscious

I am tired of being "coonscious," painfully aware of the expectation that I navigate white patriarchy while appearing black enough. I am so tired of managing mainstream culture while trying to manage being black and the inherent ways it requires me to act—act grateful, white, or happy about everything, even the atrocities. I'm exhausted by the ways it requires me to take up acting!

On the other hand, I wonder how I could not be black enough. I don't have the ability to pick up and put down my blackness. I am just—Black!

My blackness can't be found in my diction or willingness to silence myself so others feel comfortable.

Some would say that is my white face or clown face. It's the mask I wear and the performance I give each day—it's my code switch!

I'm tired! I'm tired of being "coonscious," painfully aware of the balance I am called to strike as I navigate this culture and climate while navigating this culture and climate.

Another way I experience "coonsciousness" is all the ways I am painfully aware of the criticism I receive when I fight the good fight from within the system.

They ask, "Where's your march, your picket sign, your picket line; where's your fight?"

As the pendulum swings, it worsens. One moment there's a public outcry for my pain and persecution. The next minute I'm warned not to play "the card."

Who's playing cards? I didn't know this was a card game. This is my LIFE!

Please tell me how to be a woman, black and hopeful, when I see how crisis abounds, the ways I'm uncovered, and how the wheels of justice have come to a screeching halt!

Please help me understand to what aim are your criticisms, expectations, and standards?

All my life I've had to manage narratives like, "You acting smart."

Why is it an act? Why don't I get to claim it as my own?

"You acting like you think you somebody!" Why is it an act? Why can't I claim my personhood? Didn't the constitution fix that?

Sometimes, I have even heard, "You're acting white!"

How is that possible?

As black as I am, as black as my problems are, could I really ever be anything but black?

I know someone who literally revels in her ability to take black people down a peg. Ever since she said this out loud to me, I have wondered about the aims of her consistent willingness to provide me with constructive criticism.

I used to call this mentorship. Now I am wondering to what calling she is responding.

I'm not certain about it but am certain how debilitating being "coonscious" can be.

I think my work in this season is to consistently honor the ways in which:

- I see the world.
- I see the work.
- I see myself.
- I see the role of my strengths.
- I define advocacy.

This season, I commit to being conscious of who I am and what I bring to the table. Moreover, I release my need to be "coonscious"!

The Work:

1. Am I allowing my sense of self-worth, impact, and strengths to be externally defined? If so, by whom and why?

2. What strategies will I employ when faced with microaggression and other caustic behaviors?

3. How can I consistently center myself and not oppression in my daily life?

With these new insights or awareness, what commitment will I make to myself or others?

_____

_____

_____

_____

_____

Chapter 65: The Impact of Othering

A recent award winner said she'd spent much of her life wanting to be different. The notion of spending most of your life wanting to be someone else really resonated with me. I, too, have spent much of my life wanting to be more acceptable to others.

These days, I say, "If only I were thinner."

Growing up, I said:

- "If only I were lighter."
- "If only my hair were longer."
- "If only my lips and nose were thinner."

I didn't realize the subtle ways in which othering has impacted my identity and my perception of my value. It birthed a contorted image of me.

It was my first introduction to the "mask." It was the beginning of me running from all that I was and neglecting the gift of me.

It launched me into a love-hate relationship with "passing." I couldn't physically "pass," so I doubled down on code-switching, condemnation, and self-loathing.

I wonder how many of us spend our lives trying to pass for or be like something born from othering?

This season, I am asking why I ever thought something was wrong with me.

I am perfectly fine.

I'm okay.

This Tiffany is good.

If you have ever heard any of these things, today I say to you that you are just fine, too:

- "Why can't you be more like..."
- "I wish you didn't act like..."
- "Why do you do that? So and so would never do that!"
- "Why do you act like that?"
- "Why do you think like that?"
- "Why do you talk that?"
- "We don't do that!"

This season, I am releasing myself from all the ways othering has caused me to question my:

- worth
- value
- strengths
- limitations
- differences
- preferences
- aspirations
- disposition
- so-called aptitude
- self-efficacy
- abilities
- desires
- choices

I call bullshit on all of it!

I was never wrong for being the only thing I could be—ME!

While I could lament all the wasted years of self-doubt and regret, today, I will celebrate my awakening.

I finally realize there is a place for me in this world even if society is perpetually asking me:

- "Why are you here?"
- "Why do you look like that?"
- "Who do you think you are?"

This season, I say to the critics, "I am here because you need me. I look unique because I am! I am an answer to your problem, so let's celebrate my arrival!"

This season, I embrace me!

The Work:

1. How have I undersold your strengths, talents, and gifts?

2. How can I develop an internal sense of worth, wealth, and value?

3. What factors are contributing to my sense of worth? What positive factors can I leverage to maintain a strong constant sense of self-worth? What negative factors must I address to stop the erosion of my self-esteem?

With these new insights or awareness, what commitment will I make to myself or others?

_____

_____

_____

_____

_____

Chapter 66: The Challenges of Comparison

If you compare yourself to others, you have already lost. You have lost your greatest areas of influence, control, and power.

When we compare ourselves to others, we falsely assume that their journey should be our journey, their strengths should be our strengths, and their life should be our life.

This coveting is dangerous! It robs us of our accomplishments, progress, purpose, and gifts.

It distracts us from our possibilities, potential, and promise.

It veils our gains.

It places a bushel over our light.

Similarly, when we compare others to stereotypes, we rob them of their humanity, individuality, and identity.

When we root our perception of others in bias, whether implicit or explicit, misconceptions and stereotypes, we rob ourselves and possibly the world of the benefits of their talents.

In our relegating, we relegate or reduce our return to the lowest denomination of our fears.

If you find yourself asking these questions, you have an opportunity to explore:

- Why is he or she always doing that or too much?
- Who does he or she think he or she is?
- Why is everyone always praising him or her?

If we find ourselves asking these questions, we should pause and ensure that we are not really asking:

- Why don't I have the courage to do that?
- Why aren't I taking the chance?
- Why don't I believe in myself more?
- Why aren't I betting on me?
- Why am I feeling undeserving?
- Why am I feeling insecure?

If we don't do this vital work, we fall prey to self-sabotage and destructive coping mechanisms like:

- projection
- gaslighting
- manipulation
- lies

We also reinforce our fears and contribute to our feelings of unworthiness.

Moreover, we victimize others by trying to confine them to narratives that distract from our work.

Rather than doing the work of developing self-esteem, setting and maintaining boundaries, and advocating for ourselves, we will vilify others who have boundaries, stand up for themselves, and celebrate their wins.

This is counterproductive and destructive to ourselves and others!

This season, and every day after, I will not covet, and I will not fall prey to someone else's covetous actions. I will honor, celebrate, and embrace my journey while I empower others to do the same.

In this next season, go live your life and welcome me living mine!

The Work:

1. How can I go beyond social comparison and establish meaningful internal standards for myself and my progress?

2. How will I identify when I have become externally focused and distracted from my growth? How will I renew my focus on my growth, needs, and areas of influence?

3. What will I do to ensure I am not resorting to destructive coping when I am feeling inadequate? What positive commitments can I make to myself and others as I strive for success? What can I do to ensure I don't fall prey to social comparison?

With these new insights or awareness, what commitment will I make to myself or others?

_____

_____

_____

_____

_____

Chapter 67: It's Time for Me to Leave the Circus!

I have found myself in situations that feel like:

- walking a perpetual tightrope, often without a safety net.
- being in relationships with people who feel like being in relationships with lions, tigers, and bears, which leaves me continuously trying to "tame" situations by setting boundaries and giving ultimatums.
- showing up as a clown, masking who I am and wearing costumes, constantly trying to perform myself into worth, acceptance, or love.

I am realizing I was never the ringmaster of these complex conditions and situations, but I can leave them!

As we begin a new season, I am leaving the circus of living out or down to other people's expectations, generational pathology, and thinking or behaviors that no longer serve me! I am trying something new!

The Work:

1. Where might I be participating in chaos or support confusion in my life?

2. In what relationships are distress, discomfort, or disease consistently occurring? How can I acknowledge these counterproductive dimensions and address them?

3. Where and why am I masking my true self? How will I commit to authenticity moving forward? What daily practices will I employ to ensure authentic living?

With these new insights or awareness, what commitment will I make to myself or others?

_____

_____

_____

_____

_____

Chapter 68: Over

Have you ever been over?

Over it?

Over them?

Over this?

This season, I am committed to being over—an overcomer!

I will not allow it, them, or things to overcome or overwhelm me.

I will not succumb to what others, things, or situations would wish to subject me to.

I will not be the subject of other people's ire, projection, misplaced anger, and frustration.

I will not change who I am to be who stereotypes, fears, and misconceptions need.

I will not allow my reputation, peace, or joy to be consumed by someone else's fears.

It's time-out for microaggression, character assassination, and other people's skewed imagination!

This season, I overcome!

No more looking over my shoulder or over simple things a half-dozen times in fear, as others are pushed to tiptoe around pink elephants, gossip, and untruths.

No more overcompensating for the confusion, chaos, or backhanded compliments.

No more working overtime to meet expectations others will never allow me to meet.

It's time-up and time-out for chasing moving targets, going down the rabbit holes others dig, and responding to the peanut gallery.

I'm over; overqualified for the drama, overdue for peace, overextended in my ability to swallow things, pretend with others, or act as if it's not happening.

I'm over, over it!

I'm over, over:

- it
- making excuses
- my destiny
- me

I'm overcoming!

I control my emotions. I exercise my choice. I decide what effect it has on me. Accordingly, I am committing to maintaining control over my emotions, decisions, and responses.

This season and every day afterward, I'm over—an overcomer.

The Work:

1. Have I given myself permission to let "it" be over? Have I accepted that the situation, relationship, trauma, or behavior can end? Am I allowing for an ending that doesn't require me to end myself, be miserable, or feel guilty for ending the problem?

2. Am I allowing myself to feel responsible for things, situations, or people for which I have no control, duty, or responsibility? Am I trying to bring solutions to issues that are not a problem?

Have I allowed an issue to become a distraction from the things you can control? Am I hiding behind problem-solving for others?

3. Am I able to accurately identify the factors at play and appropriately address them? Have I explored and ruled out:

   a. Being in a toxic or hostile environment
   b. Narcissism
   c. Codependence
   d. Enmeshment
   e. Depression
   f. Anxiety
   g. Other factors that may require formal intervention

With these new insights or awareness, what commitment will I make to myself or others?

_____

_____

_____

_____

_____

Chapter 69: Is the Gas Light On?

I've been struggling with the need for clarity. I feel like I need something to stay clear, clear about:

- what is happening
- clear about my role in it
- clear about why it is happening
- clear about what to do about it
- clear about the aims, intentions, and purpose of the person doing it

I think I need a carbon monoxide detector or a smoke detector. Maybe I need both.

I need something that will detect the odorless bad intentions that show up as lowered expectations and ceilings on my aspirations.

I also need a smoke detector for those who dare bring smoke! I want to learn to firmly say, "Stop the smoke and set the mirrors down!"

Unfortunately, I'm not sure I even know when it is happening until after it has happened.

Mostly, I want to practice trusting my discernment, intuition, and gut feeling. They have never steered me wrong. Unfortunately, in the windstorm of gaslighting, I find myself quieting them, which leaves me disquieted.

Gaslit, I will literally take the batteries out of what my eyes are seeing, my ears are hearing, and my heart is feeling.

Gaslit, I am subject to peril, allowing the unconscious or conscious ism to burn my hopes down.

I can't quite put my finger on it, but something feels unclear.

Just when my heart is feeling, my eyes are seeing, and my ears are hearing, there's the soft peddling of subtle innuendo, mistruths, and stereotypes.

There's the "divide and conquer" that has me thinking I'm just trying to bridge a divide but its intention is to facilitate my conquest, my defeat.

There's no overcoming, even for the overcomer, because I have misunderstood the game and its aim.

This season, I will commit to trusting my knowing, standing in my truth, and prayer. I want to know how to turn the gaslighting off.

The Work:

1. How can I identify when gaslighting is occurring and implement a constructive approach?

2. How do I maintain clarity and stay in touch with the reality of the situation when gaslighting is occurring?

3. How can I maintain boundaries and psychological safety in the face of gaslighting? What can I do in the moment? What action is needed in the long term?

With these new insights or awareness, what commitment will I make to myself or others?

_____

_____

_____

_____

_____

Chapter 70: Gossip as a Vehicle of Shame

Be careful about what spreads in gossip. It isn't just the story that is retold. Shame spreads too. Judgement accompanies it too, a judgement that imprisons the gossiper.

It is a double-edged sword that cuts both ways. It injures everyone around. It injures the person whose story is being transported to and fro. It injures the person transporting someone else's story as they lose the trust of the hearers and are subtly imprisoned in the judgement they foster. They throw a net of shame, judgement, and veil of perfectionism over everyone at the water cooler.

When we gossip, we spread shame. Unwittingly, we also handcuff ourselves to perfectionism and fear. By spreading other people's failings and flaws, we also seed untenable standards in our own lives.

It's impossible to say to others, "You won't believe what happened to so and so," without creating the expectation that it can't, won't, or shouldn't happen to us.

Recognizing this paradox, I now realize that grace also spreads. When I give others grace, I give myself grace; even if it is just the grace of knowing that others are not talking about me.

Accordingly, it is important to realize the ways in which gossip becomes a vehicle for shame in our lives and others. What is seemingly innocuous, is actually cancerous in organizational cultures, family systems, and friend circles.

We must actively guard against it in this society where everything has the potential to go viral.

In the wake of my failure, shame spread. It was in the whispers near the water cooler, in the darting eyes and the disingenuous smiles.

It betrayed me but it also betrayed others. The carriers of gossip thought they were merely spreading my heartbreak, they didn't realize that in their gossip were chains, the chains of perfectionism.

With each snide remark, in the wave of gloat, was the prison they were creating for themselves. Even more insidious are the ways gossip distracts and paralyzes. It distracts from the ownership we can take in our own lives.

The Work:

1. How can I acknowledge and address the deleterious effects of gossip?

2. What practices, strategies, and boundaries can I adopt to maintain psychological safety in the face of the toxic culture gossip fosters?

3. How can I be an advocate and accountability partner when gossip is fostering a toxic climate?

With these new insights or awareness, what commitment will I make to myself or others?

_____

_____

_____

_____

_____

Chapter 71: The Cowardly Chickenhearted

Have you seen the cowardly chickenhearted?

They hang out in flocks. They have the same feathers as they jolly in flocking together.

They cower near water coolers, whispering about:

- each other when they are not together?
- about you and me when they are in numbers
- themselves in their hearts and heads
- about everything but solutions to problems, change, and ideas

They cluck about and hope you can't see that they are afraid of flying, they are scared of trying, and they are unsure about their wings.

They peck and peck mostly at things on the ground. They never uplift. Their communication is not sound.

Relegated to hatching eggs that never birth, eating seeds on dirty turf, their days are spent clucking about and pretending that they have all the clout.

As I ponder the plight of the cowardly chickenhearted, I pray they'll see beyond the coop. I pray they realize they were never meant to stoop, stoop as low as tearing others down. I pray they'll uplift and finally get off the ground.

Until then, I'll pray to change the flock. I'll pray for the head cock. At a minimum I'll pray they finally take stock of how their words shame and hurt, and ultimately keep their reputation in the dirt.

The Work:

1. How can I foster a positive culture and healthy climate in the face of toxicity?

2. How can I support authenticity and transparency as a strategy for mitigating toxicity?

3. How can I support safe spaces in toxic climates?

With these new insights or awareness, what commitment will I make to myself or others?

_____

_____

_____

_____

_____

Chapter 72: The Masquerade Ball

Recently, I saw a group of individuals as they are. First, I lamented losing who I had believed them to be. Then I feared all the ways I had let them in when I thought I knew them. I could not unsee what I had seen of them. I could not hide from the reality of their beliefs. Most troubling, I could not hide myself from their beliefs.

In something akin to a masquerade ball, I saw several individuals recently. For a fleeting moment, they laid down their masks, and I saw them.

Perplexed, I have asked myself what I can do. What can one really do with someone who is other than you believe them to be?

Surprisingly, when we are not prepared for what we come to know about others, we may:

- lie to ourselves about who they really are
- pretend with them
- bury our heads in the sand
- secretly operate from distrust instead of acknowledging that your trust has been shaken

Having watched some pretend it didn't happen and secretly distrusting their intentions for others, I am now exploring what can be done with distrust.

The complexity of the issue called into question all I thought I knew about them. It was as if behind their neatly adorned masks, I saw their hearts, their true intentions, their judgment, and their careless regard for other people's feelings.

Stunned, I paused and reflected. It was as though we'd been dancing at this masquerade ball, but I never really knew them. I began to wonder about their music sheet, style of dance, and the intent of their dance invitation.

Feeling emotionally betrayed, I waited for their apology, their acknowledgment, or some repair.

Instead, they retorted with condemnation. Figuratively they said, "This is a masquerade ball. Why are you looking at my real face?"

Still, another said, "My silence betrayed me. I know I am masquerading. I'm not always sure how to cover the parts of me that know better."

In this moment, I realize I am struggling too. I don't know how to pretend that I didn't see them. I also don't know how we've danced together without agreeing to the music or the style of dance.

Equally troubling is the line dancing underway. There is something insidious underway in response to the unmasking. Someone said, "Maybe that's not who you saw. You can never be sure of your eyes."

Someone else said, "I see them all the time, but I don't know what to do about the makeup they ask us to wear."

What is the resolution in these instances?

Does everyone take their masks off so you know whose invitation you have accepted? Or with whom you are subject to dance?

Do you ban masquerading?

Do you say, "You have to clean up your face, e.g., feelings, intentions, and judgment."

Like most things, some will say there is no easy answer. I just believe it should be easy to say no to masquerading.

The Work:

1. How can I maintain my authenticity in environments characterized by duplicity, mystification, or dishonesty?

2. How can I honor my intuition in the face of deception, manipulation, and/or gaslighting?

3. What strategies can I employ to mitigate the impact of toxic environments, narcissistic practices, and mystification?

With these new insights or awareness, what commitment will I make to myself or others?

_____

_____

_____

_____

_____

Chapter 73: Hung from the Ladder

Have you ever been hung from the ladder? Ascended to a height beyond your wildest dreams and left precariously dangling?

It's true that the air feels thin at the highest heights. So when you take a deep breath, you gasp.

From the top of the ladder, you remember every rung, and in the fall, you begin to question every step.

While dangling, you wonder how long you can hang there. You contemplate whether it's better to risk the fall or the strangulation.

In time, you realize there is no easy answer. Later, you realize no one is coming. Still, later, you wonder why no one came.

First, you look inward. You ask where you went wrong. You ask what you could have done differently. You ponder why you weren't enough.

Then, you look outside of yourself. You ask about the bag you are holding. You realize you were never given the rules they play by. You stare at the cards, but you don't play them.

Instead, you join others in blaming you. You apologize a lot.

When you are stronger, you:

- ignore the whispers
- forgive yourself
- try again
- own what you can
- live by the serenity prayer
- hold onto the lesson but let go of the shame

Hopefully, you climb again.

If you do, do so with the wisdom of knowing that nothing is forever, neither the failure nor the win.

The Work:

1. How can I make peace with this experience?

2. Do I know what this experience came to teach me? How do I acknowledge those lessons? How will I use those lessons to grow?

3. How will I find, value, and apply the lessons gleaned from this experience?

With these new insights or awareness, what commitment will I make to myself or others?

_____

_____

_____

_____

_____

Chapter 74: Still Threatened?

It had been so long that I had forgotten it could be so overt. Because it is a subtle backdrop to my daily existence, I had forgotten that it can slap you in the face.

Today, someone locked their car doors as I walked past.

I was astounded.

There I was, passing in my Sunday best, hopeful about the young people I would soon see and thankful to be seen again.

And then, it happened.

Someone saw me in the ways that break my heart, in the ways I can't seem to get beyond.

I try and stand, but still, I fall prey; prey to misconceptions, stereotypes, and misgivings.

Try as I might, no amount of education, straight hair, heeled feet, pressed garments, or a big smile can save me.

Trapped, instead of freed by my work ethic, my character, and my genuine care for humanity, I cried in my car.

I used to get mad, really mad. I'd say, "I'll prove them wrong! I'll show them. I'm good enough!"

Now, I just cry most days because I'm tired.

I'm so tired of managing fragility, trying to make room for more than patriarchy, fighting just to stand in my femininity, and just trying to live as Tiffany with a little dignity.

I speak my truth. Then others say, "I pray for you," they pray for things like:

- my strength because they know it's not going to change, so they pray I'll endure
- my protection because people get in trouble for telling the truth or setting boundaries
- my peace because they know it's disturbing to be treated this way and witness this treatment every day
- my heart because they know this hurts, is heartbreaking, and is meant to break me, even if it's just breaking me down

Today, I exited the parking lot, with my windows rolled down, in the rain. I wanted her to see me.

I cried when I realized that I believed that she would see me differently if she saw my car. I realized how much I put on for the others that other me.

I cried when I realized my sons and daughters don't have this car, this education, my track record, just their humanity.

I cried because I knew our humanity was not enough.

I thought, "Somehow, I'm still 3/5ths, but all of her fear. How could this be?"

Then I remembered how everything gets magnified through the lens of fear, hate, and the lies we tell ourselves to maintain the things we haven't earned, the things we stole, or the ways this status quo only works if we dehumanize each other.

So today, I'll cry a little more. I'll grieve the loss of my delayed arrival. I'll maintain my peace even though this prejudice leaves me in pieces.

Then, I'll remember I am whole, wholly adequate, wholly worthy, and wholly good enough. And then, I'll remember that is why I was threatening.

The Work:

1. Am I conflating other people's bias with my worth?

2. What can I do to maintain my psychological safety in climates characterized by bias and oppression?

3. What safeguards can I put into place to protect myself from internalizing these biases?

With these new insights or awareness, what commitment will I make to myself or others?

_____

_____

_____

_____

_____

Chapter 75: Go Where You Are Needed!

Last night, I attended a convening where someone remarked, "We must go where we are needed."

It compelled me to consider the narratives we hear about belonging, work, and purpose.

In recent years, others have said:

- "Go where you are celebrated!"
- "Don't stay anywhere where you are just tolerated."
- "I want to be where I am appreciated."

What do you do when your calling has you serving in places where you are needed but not wanted?

Even more nuanced is this challenge of navigating spaces where only parts of you are desired.

If you began your professional journey when I did, you received clear messages about checking things at the door, including your emotions, your problems, your needs, and possibly your identity. Moreover, the standard for leadership was modeling male-centric depictions of leadership.

Even more complex was an ongoing debate about whether persons of color possessed the aptitude to hold leadership roles.

I distinctly remember being assigned books in college like *The Bell Curve: Intelligence and Class Structure in American Life* and *The Second Shift: Working Families and the Revolution at Home*. These books examine the complexity of gender and race, while subtly highlighting the ways in which we accord and maintain variations of privilege.

This season, I am unpacking these messages, while exploring how I can be in places where I am needed but not wanted.

After years of contorting, code-switching, and masking, I am finally exploring how much or how little of myself I am willing to bring to other people's problems in hopes of being part of the solution.

I am exploring whether I can really be the change I want to see in the world and at what cost.

I think it has taken me this long to explore this conundrum because I didn't feel I was entitled to complain.

After all, so many fought for me to have basic privileges as a woman and person of color. So, I have consistently told myself that I'm just paying my dues.

In some ways, I think I may be exploring the broader question, "How much is enough?"

Painfully, my first job included someone telling me to place their change on the counter because they didn't want me to touch their hand. In the second week of my doctoral program, someone said it's a known fact that Blacks commit more crimes without any retort.

I'm still living down the ways I feel expendable and the misconceptions that impact my experience, such as the belief:

- that I can tolerate more
- that I don't need as much
- that I will work more and for far less than others
- that my brilliance is an anomaly
- that I am playing cards when I ask about parity, inequity, or disparity
- that I am inherently angry and not perpetually traumatized

I think this season is about acknowledging these unspoken beliefs, being honest about their toll, and mitigating where I can.

I am also acknowledging that my shoulders aren't broad enough.

Another epiphany is my recognition that there are several animals I no longer want to be likened to:

- a workhorse
- a black sheep
- a mule

There are also several animals for whom my patience is exhausted, including snakes, glory hogs, dogs, chickens, and chameleons.

In this vein, I have also decided that there are some inanimate things we should not consent to being, such as a whipping post.

Some days I'm even tired of being a sounding board.

Moreover, I no longer believe I am meant to carry everything, especially not shame, guilt, or the expectation that I can be everything to everyone.

This season, I'm going to get clear about "how much" I'm going to pay. Off the table are my humanity, dignity, and peace.

Historically, I have taken whatever was handed to me, including taking responsibility for making others feel better about how they mistreat me.

This discounting of my soul, my worth, and my existence has been debilitating and is no longer sustainable. In this moment, I am acknowledging that it is too much.

As a "first," we tell ourselves that this degradation is the price we pay for progress. What if you are the 20th, the 4th, the 10th, or the 1,000th? Shouldn't it be cheaper, safer, or more obvious that I belong?

What if you have been doing a second shift all of your life, marriage, generation, or existence? Shouldn't it be clear by now that you want the same respect as any other human being, especially the right to life, liberty, and the pursuit of happiness?

Some days it feels, as much as we have grown, there are still so many rights in question, like the right to:

- choose
- life
- marriage
- equal pay
- being safe while we bear arms

Each of these rights and others are calling us to be in places where we are needed but may not be wanted. In some instances, they demand that we only bring parts of ourselves like:

- a blind eye
- a listening ear but no voice
- patience but no expectation for change

It can all be too tiresome some days.

So this year, I am committing to a measured approach. I am reminded that someone wisely told me, "Tiffany, you don't have to set yourself on fire to keep others warm."

I am also realizing I don't have to continue swallowing the insults, transgressions, or mistreatment. I can decide to:

- have and maintain boundaries
- not participate
- change my mind
- have expectations of others

- stop avoiding, hiding, pretending, and people pleasing
- rest
- choose myself
- leave

This season and every day forward, I am going to choose!

The Work:

1. How am I honoring my right to choose? Change? Stop? Leave? Say no?

2. What can I do to consistently set and maintain boundaries needed to ensure my psychological safety? How can I strike the balance of contributing to social change while maintaining my well-being?

3. What unspoken beliefs should I address so I can begin to have a life of my choosing? How will I be sure to engage or contribute in ways that allow me to maintain my dignity and honor my humanity?

With these new insights or awareness, what commitment will I make to myself or others?

_____

_____

_____

_____

_____

Chapter 76: "Your Work Here Is Done!"

Over breakfast today, I made the declaration that I was getting out of toxic relationships. I noted how there are some people in my life that I feel worse about myself after being with them.

Initially, my insight was that I was in these unhealthy relationships because I understood that hurting people hurt others. As a dutiful friend, I thought it was my responsibility to love them through it, even though their commentary was often hurtful or critical.

I had never considered that I was choosing hurtful relationships because I was hurting. Imagine that! Imagine compounding your pain by choosing relationships that perpetuate or affirm your hurting.

At that moment, I thought, *My work here is done.* I thought I finally understood I couldn't save anyone.

Now, I realize my work here is done because I finally have the courage to save myself. I have finally found the strength, time, and space to heal—because I made the space, time, and priority out of my healing!

My work here is done because others were never the work. Other people are never the project! If you believe they are, then your work is figuring out why you are enmeshed, codependent, or people pleasing.

If they are, then your work is to figure out why it's easier to pretend that you are fixing others than to focus on the one person you can change—YOU!

If you don't figure this out, you may find yourself parenting your children well into their 50s and 60s. You may find yourself raising your spouse. You may find yourself with a cape around your neck that gradually becomes the noose of codependency.

This season and every day forward, I'm staying out of the "saving business" and I'm fixing me! I'm getting clear about the work and my role in relationships. I'm embracing a new foundational truth: "You can't be in a healthy relationship with anyone else until you are in a healthy relationship with yourself!"

This season, I'm celebrating that my work in this area is done!

The Work:

1. What work will I do to heal my way toward healthy relationships?

2. What boundaries are needed to maintain healthy relationships?

3. What work will I do to ensure my psychological, emotional, and physical well-being consistently?

With these new insights or awareness, what commitment will I make to myself or others?

_____

_____

_____

_____

_____

Chapter 77: You're on the Right Track!

If they are asking you if you are okay, you may finally be on the right track. If you are no longer pretending or hiding, you may finally be on the road to your truth.

Don't turn away!

Look your fears, hurts, and traumas in the face and acknowledge them. Being honest about their existence is the only way to heal from them.

In a culture that tells us it's bad to cry or it's weak to hurt, you may be compelled to ignore the wound or continue to patch it with bandaids.

Don't do it!

It's these half-hazard approaches to trauma that will cause you to bleed out. Moreover, if you are the first person in your family or friend circle to pull your head out of the sand or to open your eyes to long-standing dysfunction, trust the process and the view! That IS everyone's bottom you are seeing and some dark things. However, this is the only way to let the light in!

So, cry! That is the cleanse. Yell! You are finding your voice. Say no! You are discovering boundaries.

And all of this is OKAY!

The Work:

1. How can I continue the brave work of confronting my fears, feelings of inadequacy, and self-doubt to mitigate the impact of othering?

2. How can I confront and heal from the self-hatred that results from othering?

3. How can I consistently maintain my well-being in the face of othering by remembering its approach, aim, and purpose?

With these new insights or awareness, what commitment will I make to myself or others?

_____

_____

_____

_____

_____

As I consider the insights and awareness gleaned from this season, what commitments to myself or others am I measuring, monitoring, and adjusting as needed, to ensure my success?

_____

_____

_____

_____

_____

_____

_____

_____

_____

_____

_____

_____

_____

_____

_____

_____

_____

Fall

As I transitioned from my summer season of discontent and self discovery, I began a fall season that could only result from the growth, discovery, and insight that preceded it. The most significant lessons were the lessons on the importance of sharing the whole truth with others and acknowledging that sometimes we are learning together.

Passing on Perfectionism

One key lesson from my fall season was the realization that we pass on perfectionism when we don't:

- tell our truth
- tell the whole truth
- tell others about our mistakes

For years, I have struggled with perfectionism. More importantly, I have consistently failed to perfect the art of living without mistakes. I suspect we all do because no one is perfect. However, the realization I had this season was that I believed I had to be perfect because no one ever told me about their mistakes.

My mother and other family members only communicated their expectations and their disappointment when I failed to meet their expectations. As I grew older and learned about our family secrets, I became resentful. I resented that they were frequently telling me not to do things that I later discovered they had done.

I did not understand that in the absence of self-forgiveness or the presence of shame, we tell others to do as we say and not as we do. We also subtly communicate that perfection is possible because we neglect to tell them that we are speaking from the experience of failing sometimes. We communicate our expectations without saying that we all face challenges, make mistakes, fail at different times, have shortcomings, and are all doing the best we can most of the time. What results is a false sense that perfection is achievable.

I now realize the people in my life would be better served if I told them that I want the best for them, experience has taught me that they can be successful, and:

- They will make mistakes along the way. This is okay. It's called practice.
- They will encounter problems for which they don't have answers. This is okay. They should take their best guess. This is the only reasonable thing to expect them to do.
- They will get it wrong sometimes, and sometimes they will get it right. This is okay. It is the nature of our humanity and our lives. They will never have all of the answers, but they will have more as we try.

Learning Together

I also realize that sometimes we are learning together. Falsely, I had assumed that others were choosing not to meet my needs or share the answers. What I came to discover was that most people are:

- doing their best
- doing what they can
- doing what they know to do
- doing what time allows
- doing what is fastest

And sometimes, people are learning as you are learning. My mother didn't have all of the answers. Sometimes, she was learning too. My husband doesn't have all of the answers. He is learning too. No leader has all of the answers. They are often learning along the way too. Moreover, most people spend their lives learning.

It is likely we will never have all of the answers. Further, there are instances where the people in our lives don't know what to do, either. Moreover, there are times when things happen that no one could have foreseen, like death, illness, infidelity, tragedy, or any number of unplanned catastrophes. There are also the routine problems of life that can seem insurmountable, if you have never encountered them.

If you can allow for the possibility that others may be learning, too, and sometimes with you, grace can be found and given. As a result of this season, I am now relinquishing the need to be perfect and embracing that I will be learning the rest of my life–and that's okay.

As you read the reflections that follow, I hope you will discover some universal truths like we are all learning and no one can be perfect.

May you find the healing and transformation I found through the journey inward!

Chapter 78: When You Do the Work, You Birth a Discovery

When you do the work, you give birth to a discovery. You finally find out what's on the other side of your fears. More importantly, you discover YOU!

What begins as maybe a commitment to living a more conscious life becomes a terrifying ride of vulnerability.

I'm still in the middle of it, but I'm thankful for what I have gained so far.

After years of stuffing, bottling, and compartmentalizing, I am unpacking. The result is that I am finding myself. I am discovering what it is to be unencumbered by who I thought I needed to be for others. I am also finding things like:

- my voice
- my way
- peace
- love
- my truth
- a new season
- a new chapter
- hope

I am finding myself, a Tiffany of my choosing, one committed to balance, progress, and purpose.

More importantly, I am uncovering a deep knowing of myself. This laboring is serving to push forth a version of me that is healed.

I liken it to a rainbow of emotions. I am exploring:

- the deep blues of my grief
- the greens of my growth
- the bright yellows of joy
- the rich reds of self-love and loving
- the opulent oranges of resilience
- the indigo of intimacy
- the violets of valiance

This rainbow of emotions doesn't negate how scary the process feels, but it does affirm that it is worth it.

It's worth doing the work!

I'm not done, but I'm already certain that it is worth it. I am seeing its value in the ways that:

- I remember I have choices.
- I have peace.
- I am prioritizing my needs.
- I am experiencing an authentic connection.
- I can see the possibilities again.
- I am forgiving myself and others.

One of the greatest gifts has been realizing that some things weren't intended to harm me. I was just collateral damage. Folks were just doing the best they could—it wasn't about me.

Realizing it wasn't about me freed me. I don't have to make myself responsible for their choices.

It is empowering me to fully own my healing because I no longer see my healing as tied to their willingness to acknowledge how they hurt me or apologize.

I get to create my own resolution and decide when I have it.

It is resulting in a grace that I get to give myself. As I acknowledge that most people are doing the best they can, there is the solidarity of knowing that I am, too.

The work has me considering other possibilities like:

- They may never apologize—HEAL ANYWAY!
- It's possible to live, love, and be happy again—if I choose!
- It is possible to be more, more of myself, because I can become more resilient, wise, or strong as a result of all of the things that happened to me, including the painful things.
- I can move on, even if others, the situations, or times don't change.

If I gain nothing but the awareness of these possibilities, then it has already been worth it.

The greatest gift is realizing that on the other side of this journey is me!

The Work:

1. Who am I discovering as a result of this journey?

2. What deep knowing do I have when I allow myself to accept myself as I am, my past as it was, and my future based on what I have already proven I can do?

3. What insights, lessons, or gifts have made this journey already worth it?

With these new insights or awareness, what commitment will I make to myself or others?

_____

_____

_____

_____

_____

Chapter 79: A "Work in Progress" Is Progress!

Over the course of this journey, there were days when I did not write. By the end of the next day, I would worry that I was failing to make progress.

In one instance, it had been a full seven days, and I was tired. In the days that preceded the stop, I had done much. I had completed many things, except giving myself:

- rest
- time
- credit
- space

I feared I had made a commitment to myself and was failing to keep it.

Like my pledge to exercise daily, I worried I had begun another thing for myself and was failing to keep my word to myself.

What I had not considered were some critical distinctions and needs that must be addressed.

First, I must begin honoring my need to rest. For years, I have burned the candle on both ends.

While trying to perform myself into worth, I have frequently gone without rest, a proper diet, downtime, or self-care.

I often forget that even God rested on the seventh day.

In my moments of fatigue, I would literally beat myself up by going over my perpetual "to-do" list in my mind and remarking:

- "You should be doing laundry."

- "You should be doing the dishes."
- "You should go to the gym."
- "You should clean out the closet."
- "You should clean out the garage."
- "You should clean out the car."

I never say:

- "You should go to sleep."
- "You should take a nap."
- "You should go home!"

Until now!

Now I'm going to tell myself that it is time to:

- go to bed
- take a nap
- go to sleep
- rest

Each day, I'm going to tell myself it is time to rest. No more forsaking myself. No more emptying my cup. No more working to exhaustion. This season, I commit to balance.

I am also going to begin making some important distinctions. The first is making a distinction between pausing and stopping.

I can pause for rest or reflection without believing that I have stopped or failed. A pause isn't and doesn't have to be forever.

The moment I begin again, I am making progress. Moreover, if I allow myself to pause, rest, and reflect, I am ensuring my growth. I am guaranteeing my win by allowing for the rest that is needed to sustain the work.

Accordingly, I commit to redefining my pauses as a necessary step or part of the work.

It is important to remember that a "work in progress" is progress!

Another important distinction is the difference between constant and consistent.

Nothing I do can be constant. Even my breathing is a cycle of inhale and exhale.

Unfortunately, I have conditioned myself to believe that everything must be constant or I am failing.

I have been showing up like constant and consistent are synonymous.

How does one avoid burnout if you are constantly working instead of consistently working?

As I read the definitions of constant and consistent, I am painfully aware of the error of my ways.

Constant is defined as "something that remains unchanged or unvarying over time," whereas consistent is a "steady reliable pattern or behavior."

Imagine that, imagine I have been trying to be unchanged when what I needed was to be steady!

This season, I will strive to be consistent so I can do the things necessary to make and maintain progress like:

- rest
- reflect
- rejuvenate

No more constant or incessant striving for me. I'm going to be consistent!

Lastly, I'm going to address my false belief that progress is only made on the incline.

This belief has led me to negate the progress that is made through things like:

- refinement
- practice
- trial and error
- learning, unlearning, and relearning

No journey of success has ever happened without one or more of these efforts. Moreover, in many instances, it has taken a combination of these efforts, much like an expert honing her or his craft.

Accordingly, I will embrace what my journey has been—a divine unfolding characterized by an incremental refinement of my nature and choices.

With these new insights, I firmly commit to rest, acceptance, consistency, and peace.

After all, to reach the summit, everyone takes a break!

If you are worrying about stalling, stopping, or losing ground, I strongly encourage you to review everything you have done and ask yourself if you have scheduled time to:

- Rest? If so, for how long? Also, ask yourself about the nature and quality of the rest. Was it forced, adequate, with guilt, or shame? We must strive to have consistent rest and make it restful. Physiologically, we are not designed to go without rest. Make sure you are requesting it with personal permission, adequately, and consistently!

- Refuel? Are you acknowledging and addressing that effort requires fuel? As you consider refueling, be sure to check your physical diet, emotional tank, mental health, and financial account. Each of these areas requires attention when you are striving for progress. Moreover, each of these areas can be depleted without adequate attention. If you have inadvertently stopped or stalled, be sure to rule out needing to refuel in each of these areas.

- Return? It's okay to pause when needed. Thwart being stalled or stopping by scheduling a return date and/or adjusting your calendar, project plan, or timeline by including defined breaks and return dates. Including defined breaks and returns can reduce guilt and shame while honoring the elements everyone needs to achieve success.

This season, give yourself the grace and gift of knowing that a work in progress is progress!

The Work:

1. How am I ensuring that I receive the rest needed to optimally work and sustain my efforts? Am I resting without guilt or shame? Am I giving myself permission to rest?

2. How am I refueling? Am I actively addressing each aspect of my health, including my physical health, emotional health, and financial health?

3. Am I consistently scheduling periods for rest and returning to the work? What can I do to ensure I will keep pace with my vision?

With these new insights or awareness, what commitment will I make to myself or others?

_____

_____

_____

_____

_____

Chapter 80: Where Are You Resting?

We must be intentional about where we rest. In shifting times, you may be compelled to rest in fear, doubt, or overwhelm because of the uncertainty of the time.

However, should we choose, we can rest in the knowledge that we have weathered 100% of our yesterdays.

We may also rest in other things like the promise of the time, our potential, or our strengths.

This season, I encourage others to join me in resting in the things that give us peace.

If you have a tendency to wait for the other shoe to drop, consider what may be gained by celebrating the moment.

If you've been taking a "wait and see" approach to life, consider smelling the roses today.

If you have been holding your breath through every new opportunity, opened door, or promotion, you have an opportunity to consider that life has shown you that your future can be bright.

Moreover, if you are recovering from a perceived failure, stagnation, or decline, you have the opportunity to remember that life is composed of seasons. As assuredly as winters come, so does spring!

So this season, choose to rest in the joy of your living. If you are unsure how to do this, try these steps:

1. Write a "100 Reasons to Be Grateful" list. Begin it with things like waking up today and breathing. Then, push yourself to go beyond the common reasons to be grateful and note the things that only you can celebrate. On my list, I have that I am so

grateful I survived my heart attack. I also have that I am so glad I am working in workforce development again. I even note things like I am so grateful my marriage is founded on our faith.

2. Write down your three greatest fears and cross off the ones that never happened. I was able to cross off each one. This taught me three lessons: 1) I worry about the wrong things, 2) I worry too much, and 3) I wasted the time I had for joy.

3. Write down your three greatest failures. Then cross out the ones you lived beyond. I was able to cross out each one. Even more powerful, as I wrote out how many days had passed—in some cases, it was decades—this exercise taught me there's no need to stay or get stuck on failing. I was wasting the energy I had been given to thrive.

4. Create a list of immutable facts; things that will never change. On my list is every degree I earned, the children I birthed, the good DNA I inherited, the gift of being born in the Information Age, and my strategic mind. This list taught me that there are things that no one can take away from me. As a result, I am never without something. As I began to list my innate gifts and talents, this list also taught me that I have an abundant life and that I have always been resourced, no matter my zip code or station.

This season, I encourage you to develop these four lists and rest on what you discover.

The Work:

1. Am I allowing the things that I am grateful for to remind me that I have abundance, opportunity, and favor? If not, why? How can I consistently center gratitude in my daily life?

2. Am I allowing myself to rest in the knowledge that I am capable? Prepared to respond to challenge? Accomplished?

3. Before I worry or ruminate, have I evaluated the likelihood of the outcomes I fear? Is my worry or fear reasonable? Does my worry match the risk? How can I ground thinking and actions in my resilience?

With these new insights or awareness, what commitment will I make to myself or others?

_____

_____

_____

_____

_____

Chapter 81: Don't Do It from 20%!

It is critical to give yourself the time, space, permission, and resources needed to operate optimally. While there can be social pressure to perform, we must strike the balance of ensuring we have given ourselves the resources to do so. We should be careful not to thwart our recovery or progress by returning to service before we can adequately serve.

In the wake of a heart attack, while in the throes of a turbulent transition, I found myself drowning in unrealistic expectations, social pressure, and shame. Unrealistic expectations told me I had no time to heal. Social pressure told me it was now or never for the recovery of my career. Shame told me I was undeserving of rest, recovery, or another opportunity.

As a result, I returned to a fairly new job within a week of having a heart attack and returned to my common practice of saying yes to everything.

What had not returned was my strength, belief in myself, or clarity of purpose. Even worse, I was not maintaining good boundaries, was subject to inordinate people pleasing, and was willing to do anything to prove my worth.

The result was that I operated from 20% of myself in some area of my life each day because I did not have the energy, rest, peace, or health to operate at 100%. I returned to being a workaholic and sacrificed quality time with my family, spouse, and friends—my support system. As was often the case for the people closest to me, including myself, I put them on the back burner.

I had gone back to my old belief that I could have it all, just not all at once. I wish someone had told me you really can't have anything when you are operating from so little—little peace, little rest, little hope, little confidence; so little of myself.

In hindsight, I wish I had given myself time to heal, not only physically but emotionally, too. While I had not missed any opportunity during that time, I had missed the opportunity to really demonstrate my potential and talent for impact.

With my new awareness and commitment to claiming the lesson from every loss, today I give myself permission to do what is needed! This includes maintaining balance, smelling the roses along the way, choosing my battles, choosing myself, setting boundaries, and saying no.

I will no longer do anything from 20% of myself. The adage that every little bit counts is false. It doesn't when you haven't given yourself time to heal. It doesn't if you've spread yourself thin or pooled all your resources into areas that don't matter in the long run.

If you are spending your time trying to live up to or down to other people's expectations, you are putting your resources in the wrong place.

If you are placing your support system on the back burner, you are placing your resources in the wrong place.

If you are prioritizing accomplishments over health, peace, love, or the things you need to operate optimally, your priorities are in the wrong place.

This season, give yourself permission and time to heal.

The Work:

1. Are my priorities in the wrong place? If so, how can I properly align them with my needs? What action will I take to maintain alignment?

2. Are my resources in the wrong place? Am I investing my time, talents, and focus in the places that ensure me maintaining well-being?

3. How can I give myself permission to rest, heal, or maintain adequate boundaries? What will I do to empower myself to prioritize my needs? How will I ensure that I am supported to perform optimally?

With these new insights or awareness, what commitment will I make to myself or others?

_____

_____

_____

_____

_____

Chapter 82: Normalizing a New To-Do List

As you begin a new week, consider normalizing a new kind of to-do list. Often our lists focus on tasks to ensure we meet work demands. What if your list also included things like balance, peace, or health?

How might your life, health, or perspective change if your list included the things you need to operate optimally?

In the weeks to come, consider including you, your needs, and at least one of your wants on your to-do list!

With an eye toward sustainable leadership, growth, and health, include:

- daily meditation
- affirmation
- love
- hope
- gratitude
- peace

This may feel lofty, idealistic, or aspirational, so let's operationalize it!

This week my daily to-do list included:

- beginning my day in prayer and meditation (daily meditation)
- concluding my day in gratitude for all the grace, gains, and gifts of the day (gratitude)
- surrounding myself with loving people, thoughts, and practices (love)
- being hopeful by remembering the ways that my efforts pay off when I try and my ability to change my situation (hope)
- sitting and sleeping in silence; no television, no radio, no distractions—just me, my thoughts, and my spouse, in the quiet of our minds and home (peace)

This work week, I accomplished this to-do list each day and substantially increased my productivity!

By beginning my day in prayer, I successfully centered each day in empowering beliefs like "I am well able," "all things are working for my good," and "I was made for such a time as this."

By concluding my day in gratitude for all that happened and all I accomplished, I was gifted a list of accomplishments each day. It empowered me to shift from saying "I had to" to saying "I got to." As a result, I began owning my day instead of feeling like it was owning me.

By surrounding myself with loving people, thoughts, and practices, I began insulating myself from people and conditions that were previously crushing.

It was like having an umbrella during a storm. It neutralized the people who willfully prod from their insecurity while empowering me with a counter-narrative for my fears. I couldn't believe I had been isolating all these years and missing the benefit of leaning in—leaning into my safe places and support!

Similarly, by reminding myself that I had survived 100% of my yesterdays, I began to thrive—thrive from the power of realizing my efforts matter and make an impact.

Imagine remembering each day that you are the kind of person who can go from dropout to doctor! It's a game-changer!

This week, when I sat in silence, I began to notice things.

I noticed my breathing. I noticed my husband's eyes, his smile, and his exhaustion. I noticed the beauty of our home and the life we are creating. I noticed how I made someone feel when I asked them if they were still showing up as old versions of who they thought others needed them to be. I noticed that I hadn't heard from my friend in two days, so I called and discovered they had lost a former spouse.

I began to notice life, the people in my life, and me!

With the gift of this new to-do list, I pray you discover yours, too!

The Work:

1. Am I on my to-do list?

2. Am I consistently prioritizing my needs, wants, and desires? If not, why? How can I consistently prioritize myself?

3. What daily practices will I commit to that ensure my growth and vision for myself?

With these new insights or awareness, what commitment will I make to myself or others?

_____

_____

_____

_____

_____

Chapter 83: Making Criticism Constructive

For years, I've been my biggest critic. So much so, that even the slightest criticism from others reverberated like a chorus. These criticisms or critiques were compounded by many subtle societal messages that served as a backdrop to my personal, professional, and leadership development.

Imagine the challenge of managing self-doubt while reconciling other people's doubt about your ability to lead because of your age, gender, weight, or culture.

This challenge can be daunting!

Criticism is inevitable but growth may not be! So it's critical to ensure that you have strategies for parsing out good feedback.

While it is true that feedback is a gift, it can also be a gift gone wrong! You may be missing the gift, if you are responding to constructive criticism by:

- ruminating
- deflecting
- projecting
- self-sabotaging
- hiding
- pretending

It's important to note that we decide whether criticism will be constructive. Like most things, how we feel, see, and respond to events is the measure of our growth, recovery, ability to compete, and ability to overcome.

If you are still revisiting a mistake you made last year, a decade ago, or last century, it's time to sit your inner critic down and say, "Get over it!"

Even more importantly, it's time to realize that the event is over and that you are deciding to extend its shelf life by going over it repeatedly. Give yourself some grace and move on. Don't be an emotional prisoner to an event that's physically over.

Another important consideration for ensuring constructive criticism is letting it in! If you deflect or project, you are marking the gift of feedback as "return to sender."

There are instances where we shouldn't receive these gifts or packages. Feedback given with questionable intent or from hurtful places requires editing. However, even in these instances, there can be a gift.

After months of working with someone who consistently maligned others in their speech and going through a range of responses, including approval seeking, I realized this person was responding from their feelings of inadequacy. Once I realized they were tearing me and others down as a way of managing their inferiority complex, I began to affirm their positive behaviors.

The lesson or gift in it for me was learning to address root causes and not just the symptoms. Addressing "my stuff" instead of projecting it onto others also became a personal standard. As a result of my many painful experiences with this person and seeing how it created a toxic culture, I got the gift of a new personal standard and practice.

In the vein of making criticism constructive, it is also important to realize when you are leveraging it as a distraction to realizing your greatness. If you receive criticism and respond to it by internalizing self-defeating thoughts, with apathy or complacency, or inaction, you may be self-sabotaging, hiding, or pretending the inevitable unredeemable failure has happened, STOP SELLING YOURSELF SHORT!

If we allow it, constructive criticism can refine us. When leveraged well, it is a honing of our skills and practice. Empower feedback in this way because it is an empowering of you!

This season, tackle your inner critic so you can topple criticism!

The Work:

1. Am I ruminating, unduly revisiting an issue whose "shelf life" has been exceeded?

2. Am I allowing the criticism I receive to be constructive?

3. How can I ensure that I benefit from the criticism I receive regardless of the critic's intentions?

With these new insights or awareness, what commitment will I make to myself or others?

_____

_____

_____

_____

_____

Chapter 84: It's My Blood Pressure! It's My Peace! It's My Well-Being!

I am committing to remembering that it is me! Ultimately, when I am frustrated, angered, exhausted, depleted, or saddened, my well-being suffers.

It's my blood pressure that's up when I allow others to move my emotional thermostat to and fro.

When I respond to the least affronts, slights, and microaggressions, it's me that is impacted.

It's my heart racing, as I try to assess the risk of the things that have me in fight or flight mode.

It puts people and situations in the driver's seat of my peace, my well-being, and even my hope.

If I'm not mindful, I will literally allow others to pick me up and drop me off emotionally, in dark places, puppet shows, and other places of their choosing.

While I have never given words to it, it's being hijacked, held hostage, and captive emotionally, literally bound by unrealized fears, unreasonable expectations, and other people's agendas.

Today, I am mindful of its physical impact, as I try to lose this stress belly and repair my heart.

It was me in the ER on the stretcher taking the Zoom call, when they said, "You're having a heart attack!"

It's likely others, too. When you hear about cancer, have you considered all the ways you have been drinking the poison of people pleasing, stress, and fear?

Have you taken account of the weight of trying to be everything and everywhere without self-care?

I think my work is to realize that I am not only emotionally impacted when I am not choosing, but I am also physically impacted.

Recognizing these impacts, I will no longer do things:

- "come hell or high water"
- "if it kills me"
- "if it's the last thing I do"

I will actively choose peace, choose myself, and let go of the things that no longer serve me.

The Work:

1. How can I be mindful of the physical impact of my emotional decisions?

2. What can I do to better manage the physical impact of my thinking and feeling?

3. What new practices, boundaries, or standards will I establish to ensure that I am addressing my well-being holistically?

With these new insights or awareness, what commitment will I make to myself or others?

_____

_____

_____

_____

_____

Chapter 85: It Wasn't a Delivery!

One weekend, I had a powerful conversation with my dearest friend. While revisiting our journey together and the numerous times we had been there for one another, we came to the powerful realization that sometimes the messages we share with others are for us, too.

There were times when we falsely believed that we were only the messenger or solely meant to impart what others may need in the moment. In hindsight, I must acknowledge that there are instances where the message I shared was also intended for me. Moreover, my ability to relate to the challenge at hand signaled that I needed to hear what I shared.

Countless times I have said to others, "You are enough" or "You will make it" while struggling with my own self-doubt. In something akin to making a delivery, I didn't realize that the package was for me, too.

What wisdom are you sharing with others? Have you considered what would happen if YOU took your word for it? Are there some timely messages you need to apply to your own life?

No doubt, we have likely asked ourselves what we would tell our sixteen-year-old self. Today, I ask you to consider what you've been telling others that you refuse to hear.

For a moment, pivot from saying "if I were you" to fully embracing the guidance that you readily give to others. Consider the things you have told your children, spouse, and friends, and ask yourself, *Are you listening to yourself?*

If you are not, ask yourself:

1. Am I leading by example or living in hypocrisy?
2. Am I telling others to live as I say and not as I do?

3. Why am I giving advice that I will not take?

The unpacking of these questions led me to some powerful existential considerations. Chief among them were:

1. Do I really believe I can and should be whole, happy, fulfilled, and in peace?
2. Do I really believe I am deserving?
3. Have I allowed myself to be content with complacency?

Also notable are the ways we know what to do when it is somebody else's story, dilemma, or problem. Amazingly, we readily affirm how others:

- will make it
- are ready
- are enough

Have you believed these things for yourself? Are you operating from the hopes and aspirations you readily affirm in others? If you are not, you have an opportunity to begin today. Moreover, the next time you deliver hope, affirmation, or belief in others, check the label. The package should be for you, too! Be sure to accept these deliveries, too!

The Work:

1. Do I embrace the advice I give to others? If not, why? Do I believe I am deserving of the success, opportunity, or hope I affirm for others?

2. Am I eschewing my own needs and challenges to support others? If so, why? Why am I neglecting my needs or problems? What can I do to make the same commitment to my well-being that I make to others?

3. How can I move beyond compassion to empathy and action? How can I consistently model the counsel I share with others? What will I do to consistently lead by example?

With these new insights or awareness, what commitment will I make to myself or others?

_____

_____

_____

_____

_____

Chapter 86: You Can't Put It On. It Has To Come From Within.

Worth can't be put on. It has to come from within.

I am acknowledging that worth isn't something you wear. It must come from within you.

While we might acquire status symbols, the most important status is the status of our hearts, minds, and souls.

When our hearts, minds, and souls are in disrepair, no title, no membership, or purchase can replace the healing needed.

Falsely, I sought affirmation from things external to me. Like being knighted, I thought I could be declared worthy. This flawed belief left me seeking approval from others and searching for value in things that could never fulfill me.

The result was worth feeling fleeting. It was falsely predicated on my ability to be what others needed.

As I grow older, I realize most people don't even know what they want.

Imagine that. Imagine the prospect of tying your sense of worth to the whims and wants of others.

Today, I am evaluating all of the things I have committed to over the years. Driven by the ideals of social responsibility and second chances, I have actively sought opportunities to help others while working to ensure systems work for the people they desire to help.

Unfortunately, I have also sought to be accepted in the absence of self-acceptance.

This is problematic. When we seek acceptance in others before we accept ourselves, there is a discounting of ourselves that leaves us used, undersold, and undervalued.

We discount ourselves and put ourselves on sale because we falsely believe we must be passing off something of little value.

This season, I apologize. I apologize to myself for not seeing me—not seeing that my value does not rest in what I can do. Rather, it is an innate characteristic of our humanity. I am, therefore, I have worth.

I also apologize to everyone that I demanded something from you that you could never give me—self-acceptance.

This season and every day forward, I remain committed to treating my sense of self-worth as the inside job that it is.

The Work:

1. Am I using external sources like public opinion, other people's perceptions or critics to determine my worth?

2. Am I substituting affiliations, memberships, or titles for self-worth?

3. Am I allowing my worth to be determined by job performance, giving, or other external factors?

With these new insights or awareness, what commitment will I make to myself or others?

_____

_____

_____

_____

Chapter 87: Collecting Baggage

This season, I'm going to make sure I'm not collecting baggage.

I am also going to unpack the baggage I've been carrying around.

This season, I'm committing to traveling light!

Essentials only!

I will no longer carry around past hurts, other people's stuff, or the weight of the apology I never got!

I'm traveling light into this next season.

I'm telling people:

- "You forgot your bag!"
- "Sorry, I can't hold that!"
- "Return to sender!"

I am checking these bags before I begin my stay; mark the ticket unclaimed!

I'm making a list and checking it twice because I'm returning these bags even if I'm not called nice!

I had bags stacked mountains high! If I were driving a stagecoach, my horse couldn't go. Some were mine but others I didn't recognize.

As I unpacked them, I soon discovered:

- a bag of unrealized dreams
- a satchel of hope deferred
- a whole case of confusion

I'm dropping these bags!

After leaving other people's bags behind, I am finding things in the pockets of my bags like love, courage, self-acceptance, and inspiration!

This season, I commit to packing light; literally, light! This year, I will live unbound!

The Work:

1. What am I carrying? Am I carrying things for others? Am I consciously or unconsciously carrying other people's hurt, trauma, or causes?

2. How can I begin to carry things that affirm, uplift, and empower? Have I made it a practice to carry things like hope, faith, and forgiveness? Am I carrying a strong sense of self-worth or self-esteem?

3. How can I be sure to delineate between what issues or baggage belongs to others and what baggage is mine to address? What will I do to prioritize addressing my baggage while recognizing that I can't change other people's baggage?

With these new insights or awareness, what commitment will I make to myself or others?

_____

_____

_____

_____

_____

Chapter 88: Be!

It's so important to push past the pretense. The older I get, the more I realize no one has it all together. More troubling, it's impossible to have it all together as social pressure and peer pressure would have you believe you can.

Even more troubling, as social media has seemingly allowed us to peer into each other's lives, the need to look great, be great, and act like everything is great has grown exponentially.

I thought the pressure would let up after each degree, each promotion, and each milestone. It didn't. The fall from grace just felt like it would hurt more.

After much reflection, I am realizing how sad it would be to spend my life:

- second-guessing myself
- pretending nothing hurts
- chasing other people's ideas of success
- wishing I was someone else
- trying to figure out who I need to be every time I meet someone
- trying to figure out who I am when I know who I am. I just don't know how to make that acceptable to everyone.

So this season, I'm committing to:

- just being
- being me
- be at peace with myself, others, and the journey

This season and every day forward, I'm going to just BE!

The Work:

1. How can I make and maintain peace with who I was, who I am, and whoever I become over the course of my journey?

2. What dimensions of myself have I been contesting? Why? What can I do to foster self-acceptance in these areas?

3. Recognizing that titles, affiliations and memberships are no substitute for self-acceptance, what will I do to maintain positive self-esteem, self-acceptance, and self-love?

With these new insights or awareness, what commitment will I make to myself or others?

_____

_____

_____

_____

_____

Chapter 89: A Muddying of the Waters

And I began to muddy the waters when I asked why.

When I asked why, things got less clear. All of a sudden, there was more than one voice. There was the voice of my mother's pain. There was the voice of my grandmother's fear. There was the silence of the bystander and the sound of the straw breaking the camel's back.

When I asked how, I heard the retelling of every attempt. There was the reverberation of all of the failed tries. The peanut gallery began to tune up. The allies rushed in but froze as I considered.

When I asked when, the timers began to sound. The cuckoo clock heckled. The calendars ran. Somewhere in the distance, the stopwatch began.

When I asked what, a debate followed. A philosopher pontificated, an orator orated, a pastor prayed, and a leader led, but we were not certain it was the way. There were definitions lying about, and there was even a construct here and there, but no certainty could be found.

After much travail, I asked who. In front of a mirror, I said, "I DO!" Gradually, a line formed. It was a group of volunteers, some solicited and some not, but each with a name or a thought.

In time, they began to shuffle and try to line up, each arguing an order based on their thought.

I cried. I fought. I exclaimed, "But what about my thoughts!"

I wondered. I wavered. I argued. I savored.

I clung to some things I'd been told. I tried to shake away the things I did not want to hold.

Finally, I left in pieces. Then, I stood in peace. Then, I fought for peace.

At first, it was just for inner peace. Then, it was for world peace. Now it's just for a piece. Tomorrow, I hope it will be for our peace.

The Work:

1. As I continue my healing journey, how can I continue to "muddy the waters' by challenging long-standing narratives, perceptions, and history?

2. What more may I gain through a practice of inquiry, reflection, and acceptance?

3. What new narratives will I foster as a result of my new clarity, resilience, and grace?

With these new insights or awareness, what commitment will I make to myself or others?

_____

_____

_____

_____

_____

Chapter 90: Are You Clear About the Race? Do You Have Reasonable Expectations for the Prize?

I wrote this reflection as I considered all the ways I had been trying to perform myself into worth. After much reflection, I realize my sense of worth, self-efficacy, and dignity should never be contingent upon anything external. Moreover, if I do not do the work of grounding my identity and worth in self-acceptance, I am easily moved by other people's opinions, agendas, and misgivings. After decades of trying to be good enough to love, I am embracing loving myself as being enough. Here's my reflection on the realization that I'm trying to be good enough instead of realizing I am inherently enough:

"As I begin a new season, I realize that I have been striving for most of my life—not in the achievement kind of way but rather contending. I am now contemplating Isaac's example and how he 'strove not!'

"Whether it's the perpetual way that I have striven to be good enough by pleasing people, or the ways I contend when I feel unseen, unheard, or misunderstood, I have been 'striving' too much!

"It has me tired! I am tired, disillusioned, and downright exhausted some days. The kind of exhaustion you would expect if you were physically wrestling, when most days I'm just wrestling with things like fear, imposter syndrome, and other people's expectations.

"I have been in a contest in hopes of winning 'best in show.' I mistakenly believed the prize was acceptance, love, or peace.

"As I begin this season, I am committing to awarding myself self-acceptance and self-love because that's the only way I can have peace.

"As I begin this season, I am getting clear about the race and the prize. There is no race! There's no contest required to be me. Most importantly, I can fully accept and love myself as I am.

"This season, I declare that I will 'strive not!'

"As I begin a new chapter or season, I invite others to consider how they are playing the game, running the race, or contending. I think there's an opportunity to redefine how one navigates their journey and rest in the knowledge of their sufficiency.

"May each season be a season of peace, joy, and acceptance, even if it's just accepting the things one cannot change, changing the things one can, and knowing the difference."

The Work:

1. Are there areas in my life where I am contending? If so, where am I contending? Why am I contending in these areas? How might I reframe the issue or understand the need in ways that allow me to cease contending?

2. Am I striving for an acceptance that only I can give—self-acceptance? What is the root of this lack of acceptance or my earliest memory of inadequacy? How might I find acceptance by acknowledging my worth?

3. Am I maintaining relationships or situations that require me to perform or give for acceptance? Am I attempting to perform myself into worth? How can I begin centering my intrinsic value in my daily life? What steps am I taking to affirm my intrinsic value?

With these new insights or awareness, what commitment will I make to myself or others?

_____

_____

_____

_____

_____

Chapter 91: Don't Strike the Rock

In recent weeks, my year-long commitment to reflection has led to great spiritual growth. While exploring the challenges of change management during executive leadership training, I was reminded of the story of Moses. Here's my reflection on Moses' journey:

Don't Strike the Rock

Moses was called to lead a people out of bondage. Despite overcoming great challenges during his tenure, he never fully realized the promise of his calling.

This failure was not the result of the feasibility of the task, a failing average, or even a lack of vision. Rather, Moses failed to temper his approach.

Moses neglected the approach that had been proposed for the task. He struck a rock instead of speaking to the issue, and as a result, he never entered into the promise of his tenure.

As leaders, we are often confronted by some of the challenges Moses faced, including:

- low morale
- self-doubt
- resistance
- obstacles
- lack of resources

Any one of these challenges can feel insurmountable and/or encumber our ability to realize our vision. As I consider Moses' leadership journey, I am mindful that:

- We can not neglect organizational morale.

- We can not let our need to prove ourselves drive our decision-making.
- We must remain resolute in our focus, lest we lose sight of the goal.

Throughout his tenure, Moses faced bouts of low morale. Each of these instances is an opportunity to explore the impact and role of the leader in these times. Having led throughout the pandemic, I can attest to the ways in which narrative, momentum, and truth become contorted in the grips of fear. If you are a leader experiencing low organizational morale, address it. The morale of an organization is the foundation of its resolve, belief, and hopes. When morale is low, so is the organization's execution. Just as planting a seed in fertile ground can be fruitful, planting innovation in an organization experiencing low morale can be the death of possibility.

Similarly, when we allow ourselves to be driven by proving, we fall victim to a God complex that will surely derail the work. No effort can be sustained or optimally executed if we are proving:

- ourselves right
- others wrong
- there's only one way
- there is no way

Moreover, we destroy our ability to partner and, thus, ensure our failure.

Lastly, Moses' leadership journey underscores that it is wholly possible to win many battles and lose the war when we are not consistently attending to our approach, communication, and goal. After bringing a generation out of enslavement, through a perilous trek, and near their goal, Moses failed to bring the people into the promised land. He lost sight of the game plan. He allowed doubt and other factors to drive his strategy. We must allow wisdom to prevail. Our strategy must be driven by what the situation demands, not our wavering or doubts.

With this new awareness, I encourage you to consider how you are leading in your home, on your job, and in your community.

In these uncertain political times, are you reminding others that they have a voice? Are you cheerleading your household to victory? Are you empowering your colleagues to transformation?

Are you resolute in your resolve?

If you are unsure or struggling, take these important steps with me:

1. Remember the mission! Oftentimes, the mission is not one instance or person. Accordingly, don't let one person or incident take you off mission.

2. Recommit to strategy. Take the time to review the strategy underway. Confirm that the strategy is the most responsive course of action and not a reaction to your fears. Once confirmed, focus on taking the next necessary step.

3. Return to executing the game plan. Take the next step. After faltering or doubting yourself, you may be tempted to ruminate—DON'T! This is where your short-term memory is needed. Grieve the delay or mistake, and move on! Once you have the lesson, there is no need to focus on the loss. Reserve that energy for moving forward!

The Work:

1. What am I doing to consistently address morale? My morale? Morale in my household? Morale in my organization? Morale in my community?

2. How am I ensuring that my leadership is responsive?

3. How am I evolving my thinking, practices, and leadership to ensure my success and the success of those I steward?

With these new insights or awareness, what commitment will I make to myself or others?

_____

_____

_____

_____

_____

Chapter 92: What Is This Moment?

As my journey unfolds, I realize that it is critical to ask, "What is this moment?"

In times of silence, I can be tempted to:

- assume "it" is over
- assume the time has passed
- assume he, she, or it has changed
- begin waiting for the other shoe to drop
- hold my breath
- assume it is someone else's time or turn

In doing so, I may:

- miss an opportunity
- neglect to do the personal development that is needed
- fail to make a decision
- fall into complacency or apathy

I may even miss an opportunity to rest or plan. Even more concerning, I may fail to realize when I am living a cycle of abuse and have entered the honeymoon period. Equally worse, I may be enmeshed, codependent, or subject to the whims of a narcissist. Either way, there is value in asking, "What is this moment?"

In asking, I have discovered things like:

- rest
- a new season
- the need for a new vision
- a new opportunity
- the end of a season or relationship

Moreover, I realize that my greatest times of challenge have come when I didn't evaluate the moment and choose an appropriate strategy.

Sometimes, I had been called to rest but I was striving ceaselessly.

One time, I was in an unhealthy relationship, and the honeymoon cycle had begun. Mistakenly, I thought things had changed or the abuse was over. I had missed an opportunity to leave.

In another instance, I had a clear awareness of needing to make a change but had misinterpreted the silence as a sign that things were going to be okay. Things were okay only after I acted. So not only had I delayed my progress, but I had also lost time when I failed to discern the moment.

Another moment greatly helped by discerning the moment is realizing when your discomfort is the result of doing something new or unfamiliar.

There have been times when I thought, "This doesn't feel right."

It wasn't that things were wrong, but rather I had no context for what was happening. Only after I persisted did I see that I was doing the right thing for me or that things would work out.

Some tangible examples of this include:

- being a first-generation college student
- starting a new business
- being a "first"
- breaking a generational curse

During each of these moments, I worried and wondered and sometimes stopped. I wish I had discerned that it was just the pain of growing.

Another critical moment to discern is realizing when many have been called to address an issue. Falsely, we can assume that there's only room for one person, program, or approach when we are addressing social issues or community needs.

The result is that we fight over the one perceived seat and neglect the rest of the table.

Rarely does the solution to a social issue or community need to rest with one person or program. That's like believing that there can only be one hamburger and that it must be a McDonald's style of hamburger.

In these moments, it is critical for us to discern that there is room for everyone! If we don't, we may:

- fail to bring our talents and strengths to the table because we believe only one person can do something
- demonize or minimize others attempting to help because we are responding from a false sense of competition
- inadequately address an issue by limiting our response to one approach or one person's thinking

In either case, we potentially limit ourselves or others.

Similarly, we must also discern when our season or role has ended. I liken this to a relay race where it is critical to know when your leg of the race has ended. I have seen this missed opportunity show up as founder's syndrome and other challenges in succession planning.

I distinctly remember times when successful leaders failed to pass the baton or wrestled with the handoff because they falsely believed that:

- things had to be done a certain way
- things had to be done their way
- there was no other way
- there was only their way
- their time was the pinnacle

Truthfully, none of these things are true. Equifinality suggests that there are multiple ways to arrive at the same place. Moreover, legacy and perpetuity dictate that we get comfortable with others continuing the work and even eclipsing our efforts.

Wouldn't it be sad to pray that the work continues and be the reason it dies because you didn't realize when the moment was calling for someone or something else?

Accordingly, as I begin a new season, I am committed to discerning the moment. With intention, I am asking, "What is this moment?"

Whether it is time to rest, act, lead, or leave, I am committed to responding accordingly.

The Work:

1. What strategies can I use to discern and appropriately respond to different moments?

2. How can I identify, acknowledge, and work through the discomfort that comes with moments like learning or new challenges?

3. How can I identify and appropriately support when the moment is calling for succession?

With these new insights or awareness, what commitment will I make to myself or others?

_____

_____

_____

_____

Chapter 93: Don't Get Lost in the Transition

It's critical not to get lost in transition. When a transition happens, we can become unsettled by uncertainty. In the absence of clarity of purpose, we can mistake a comma (transition) for a period (ending) or even an exclamation mark (a catastrophe).

While unsettling, if we remember our calling, the nature of seasons, and the role of perseverance, we can ensure our transition is not an ending.

During some of my most unsettling transitions, remembering my calling was stabilizing. When I leaned into the question, *What am I being called to now?* my ability to pivot and find purpose in change greatly increased.

This shift in perspective is both centering and empowering. It is a call to action, a reminder that there is more work to be done! It is also an empowering reminder that callings often span our lifespans, places, people, and situations!

Another stabilizing strategy is remembering the nature of seasons. Seasons are a foundational aspect of our experience, and transitions are often a signal of a new season ahead.

When we understand that transitions usher in new seasons, we can leverage the principles of seasons to powerfully embrace and master transitions. Some core principles of seasons are:

- They are constant.
- They are consistent.
- They can be predictable.
- They are necessary for your growth.
- They are a requisite for transformation and resolution.
- They shouldn't be avoided.

When we acknowledge that transitions are inevitable, we take the surprise out of them. Acknowledging they are constant and consistent brings a level of predictability to the seemingly unsettling. Just as our most powerful leadership experts encourage us to "begin with the end in mind," we should begin any new venture, tenure, chapter, or transition with a clear sense of our desired impact and knowledge that all things truly do come to an end.

What if we prepared for the inevitable transition with proven strategies like succession planning?

Other important dimensions of seasons and their connection to transitions are that they are necessary for growth and transformation. Every professional career and life journey can be characterized as a series of seasons, each interconnected and essential to our development.

Similarly, real change is often accomplished through a series of stages or seasons. We cannot realize our potential or solutions without the complex interplay of each season and the transitions that ensure the next stage of growth!

Lastly, we must remember not to avoid transitions. Just as removing training wheels from a bike is a signal that you have mastered bike riding, a transition can be a signal that you are ready for more! When you resist the next transition, you risk delay, demise, and deterioration. Don't get stuck!

As you experience your next transition, embrace it, embody it, and be emboldened. Remember, it's all working for our good!

The Work:

1. What am I being called to now?

2. As this season ends, what have I gained from this time? What

healing or resolution resulted? What learning or lesson was gained? How am I better as a result of this time? How has this time prepared me for more opportunities?

3. What may be gained if I embrace a new season?

With these new insights or awareness, what commitment will I make to myself or others?

_____

_____

_____

_____

_____

Chapter 94: A Tool in the Wrong Hands

Have you ever teetered between silence and frustration because you feared others were taking credit for your ideas or efforts?

Was your resolve to stop sharing because you felt used?

Believing that you could effectively contribute to the effort, did you grow frustrated as the process evolved without your contribution?

If you have ever teetered in this way, you have an opportunity to look inward.

As a strategist, systems thinker, and visionary, I thought my greatest gift was my thinking. As someone from humble beginnings, conditioned to undervalue my worth, I frequently worried about people taking credit for my ideas and work.

I now know the greater gift is my ability to freely give to my call, stand in purpose, and trust that all things are working for my good.

As a person of faith, I now know that my gifts come through me. They are not of me. My promotion, opportunities, and results have all been tied to my willingness to freely share my ideas and partner with others.

It is fear that would have us believe that there is no room for others to share in our thinking. It is ego that would compel us to fight for credit over purpose.

It is a distraction that would have us believe that others can outdo us at being ourselves, wielding our gifts, or delivering on our purpose.

Just as only Moses could wield the staff to be what was needed for his calling, only you can wield your thinking, gifts, or tools in the manner that you are called to do.

With this knowledge, commit to the power of giving yourself over to purpose.

Over the course of this year, I have revisited the notion of being a tool in the wrong hands. Central to my unpacking has been making peace with the ways I have felt used by others and the notion of working on purpose. As I have strove to unpack and address this conundrum, I have found it useful to take inventory.

I also encourage you to take inventory too. Begin by listing everything you have given. Consider the ways you have given intellectually, emotionally, physically, and financially. Once you have listed what you've given in each of these areas, evaluate what you have gained or lost.

Over time, I have discovered that I have gained things like resilience or a new skill. I have also discovered that I have lost things like time and peace. Additionally, I have discovered that nothing is a loss if I have learned.

The next time you are worried about being a tool in the wrong hands or just a tool in someone else's or an organization's hands where you may not feel mission-aligned, consider taking inventory. Our ability to consciously evaluate our contributions is a powerful tool. When wielded appropriately, it allows us to take measured action, conserve our energy and time appropriately, and work against codependence, enmeshment, and other counterproductive behavior. This season, consider your giving!

The Work:

1. What gifts will I gain if I freely give my gifts?

2. How can I shift from a scarcity mentality to find abundance?

3. How can I work to trust the process in my daily life?

With these new insights or awareness, what commitment will I make to myself or others?

_____

_____

_____

_____

_____

Chapter 95: Never Be Too Tired for Yourself

Recently, I had the privilege of breakfast with some incredible leaders. One is a prolific writer. Another is an unparalleled strategist and event planner. Still, another is an extraordinary operations leader who can bring process and structure to any organization.

I asked if they had considered how their innate gifts could elevate any organization and if they were using their gifts in other places.

Several remarked how they were frequently tired after long days at work, community service, and parenting.

It occurred to me that I spent many days tired in the same manner. What I had never considered until this moment was that I am frequently too tired for me.

As they remarked about the impossibility of finding time to do one other thing in this season, I lamented how I had spent much of my life never having time to:

- eat right; I had spent many days in drive-throughs, eating between meetings
- exercise as I ran from one project, problem, or proposition to another
- love myself while eating my emotions, wrestling with self-doubt, and prioritizing other people's needs

How is it that we can't find time for ourselves?

It also compelled me to consider what else I hadn't had time. Troubling, there were times I had not made time to:

- plan for my future
- invest in me

- forgive myself or some others
- rest or play
- dream
- pray
- meditate
- breathe
- believe again
- change

Of all the things I had not made time to do, the most problematic was not making time to continue improving myself.

Even more troubling, I had not considered how running out of time could be tied to not making time.

So today, this year, and every day forward, I will not run out of time for me. I will no longer not have time for myself. I will not get to everything on the list, but me.

I will not complete everyone else's list and fail to complete mine!

This season and every day forward, I am:

- making my list
- at the top of my list
- getting to me on the list

Even if it's just beginning my day with God in meditation or gratitude, I'm starting with me.

Even if it's just asking myself what I have done for myself today, before I ask the seventh person how I can help them. I am helping me see my way clear of people-pleasing.

Even if it's just making time for my goals as I check off the list of things I commit to do for others, I am going to achieve my personal goals as I achieve my professional goals.

I am going to have, make, and maintain time for the only me I have— ME!

The Work:

1. How will I consistently prioritize making time for myself?

2. What is my plan of care?

3. How will I hold myself accountable for the self-care needed to sustain my growth?

With these new insights or awareness, what commitment will I make to myself or others?

_____

_____

_____

_____

_____

Chapter 96: An "Overcoming Plan"

Yesterday, I attended a candidate forum where the panelists were asked, "Recognizing the challenges you will face, what is your 'overcoming plan'?"

Not until that moment did I realize I needed an overcoming plan. While I had a plan to live up to my potential, to work in purpose, and to transform the conditions that negatively impact others, I did not consider that I would still be overcoming after four degrees, several leadership appointments, and many accolades.

As I ponder this plan, I am encouraging myself and others to consider the things that must be overcome. Top of mind are:

- not being pigeonholed as an angry black woman
- being always required to have a reference or a citation for credibility because my feelings and experience are valid without someone else attesting to them
- managing other people's guilt or bias
- perfectionism and self-doubt

It's from this place that I am asking myself and others how many times they have felt overcome when it is likely that they were just overcoming things like implicit bias, micro-aggression, or misogyny.

It's from this place that I harken back to the refrain, "...we shall overcome one day!"

It's from this place that I lament the inaction and apathy that ensues from the exhaustion of having to overcome all of the time.

Today, as a first step to overcoming, I give myself permission to just be over it!

As a part of my "overcoming plan," I am over:

- having to explain that I am entitled to my feelings
- needing references and citations for my lived experiences
- bearing the emotional weight of other people's fragility or guilt
- explaining why bad behavior is bad. If we are to realize the potential of our personhood, our nation, or our ideals, it will come at the cost of our fears, bias, and prejudice.

If we are to overcome one day, it will come over acceptance, our shared sense of humanity, and a commitment to everyone's dignity.

This season, I make this commitment the foundation of my overcoming!

The Work:

1. What is my plan for overcoming old challenges when they resurface?

2. How can I remain consistent in my growth and learning?

3. What permission, practice, or perspective must I implement to ensure my continued success?

With these new insights or awareness, what commitment will I make to myself or others?

_____

_____

_____

_____

_____

Chapter 97: Remembering Your "Why" so You're Not Screaming, "Why!"

In those moments when my inner voice is screaming "Why!" It is critical to revisit and remember my why.

In those moments of distress, confusion, or disillusionment, what if we remembered:

- Why we are doing this
- What our aim is
- Why it's critical
- What we are hoping to impact
- Why it is necessary

When I forget my why and begin crying out why, these statements become criticisms and judgments that manifest as questions:

- Why are we doing this?
- What is our aim?
- Why is this critical?
- What impact were we hoping to have?
- Why is this necessary?

When I center myself on my purpose instead of my fears and frustrations, I am more clear in my intention, powerful in my impact, and grounded in peace.

I must also remember that there are appropriate times to ask myself these questions. I should ask at the beginning of any effort to ensure I have the clarity I need to execute.

I can also ask during the process because it can be an inquiry of refinement.

However, if I am crying out, "Why," if I am crying, there is an opportunity for me to look inward and rule out:

- being fearful that I am not equipped for the task
- that the goal or will has changed
- that another strategy is needed
- the wrong people are seated in the right seats on the bus; conversely, the right people are seated in the wrong seats on the bus
- that I am on the wrong bus
- that I don't want to take this trip anymore

Either way, there is some value in revisiting my intention and grounding my perspective in purpose.

I think my work here is to revisit and remember the "why" that has brought me to this moment.

The Work:

1. What is my why?

2. How can I remain diligent in leading from a place of confidence?

3. What practices, perspectives, or perceptions can be leveraged to maintain focus, health, and progress?

With these new insights or awareness, what commitment will I make to myself or others?

_____

_____

_____

_____

Chapter 98: Stewardship

Defined as the "careful responsible management of the things entrusted to your care," I had relegated "stewardship" to the tangible things in my life, like possessions. As time passes, I realize that stewardship is the careful responsible management of all the things we are entrusted with, including our talents, gifts, and relationships.

With this new framing, I am reframing how I steward things, like opportunity, second chances, and my health. I am also re-evaluating what it means to be entrusted with a challenge.

Thoughtfully, I am defining "careful management" and what it means to be responsible when you are entrusted with a spouse, children, friends, or staff. I am compelled to co-create the definitions of words like marriage, parenthood, friendship, and management in ways that allow me to steward with others.

Similarly, leadership is being redefined as I consider what it means to be given stewardship for an organization's greatest asset, its human capital.

Imagine the complexity of purporting to take charge of others while not carefully managing the most foundational aspects of your own life, such as your physical, emotional, or mental health, or sense of efficacy or integrity.

Falsely, we believe we can show up in one area of our life, in one manner, and not have it bleed over. Even more troubling is the tendency to judge others by their behavior and ourselves by our intentions.

While there is much to unpack, today, I will just consider how I am stewarding all that I have been given.

This season, I am mindful that I must:

- take account
- take ownership
- take responsibility
- take time

As I redefine stewardship, I must take account of all that I have been entrusted. Imagine being responsible for a list of items but never reading the list. In many respects, this is our plight if we have not accounted for all of our gifts, talents, assets, and relationships.

Imagine having lived a half century and still discovering new interests and skills. Moreover, imagine being in a relationship and never truly knowing your partner, friends, family, or staff.

As I reconsider stewardship, I am mindful that there must be an accounting, a recognition of all that I bring to the table and what others bring. More importantly, it must be a full accounting, the good and the bad. Otherwise, I have relegated myself and others to pretense, masks, and conditional regard. Today, I will settle these accounts and show up in gratitude for all that I am and what others have been to me.

I will also take ownership. I will fully own my gifts, talents, strengths, and weaknesses. I will also own my part in my shared journey with family, friends, and others. I will own where my choices and gifts have taken me and stop eschewing my progress as a chance. I will also accept that some may never own what they do, and that's okay because that is their work, not mine.

Today, I will also take responsibility for the areas in my charge like my feelings, actions, and perceptions. I will also release myself from feeling responsible for other people's actions, intentions, and misgivings. For far too long, I managed my life by trying to manage how others showed up. This is a trauma response that has the propensity to leave you people pleasing and making excuses for others. Today, I empower myself and others to be productively responsible.

Lastly, I will take the time I need to steward well. This includes time for self-care, patience, grace, progress, and balance.

In my effort to outrun poverty, misconceptions, and bias, I have run myself ragged. Moreover, I have let perfectionistic expectations cause me to believe that no matter how fast or far I ran, I was still behind.

Today, I release myself from this false belief. Today, I reframe how I talk about time. My new narrative for time is:

- I have accomplished a lot over time.
- My life is unfolding according to God's perfect timing.
- I have time; time to rest, time to practice, time to figure it out, and time to grow.
- Who I am becoming couldn't have happened at any other pace than this timing.
- What is happening is happening right on time.

This season, I pray others will join me in redefining stewardship. May everyone be empowered to steward.

The Work:

1. How can I continue to take account of what I have been entrusted to ensure I am taking ownership in the ways that I can and should?

2. Am I prioritizing stewarding my health, talents, and peace?

3. What is my stewardship practice and how can I ensure that it is responsive?

With these new insights or awareness, what commitment will I make to myself or others?

_____

_____

_____

_____

_____

Chapter 99: Taking a High Road with Harm

Through reflection, I realized that I have been praying about troubling people but not praying for the troubled people. This concerning awareness compels me to ask why.

If your focus is not on the betterment of others, you have an opportunity to ask why.

Recognizing this challenge, I began the journey inward by reconciling whether I had been praying about people with:

- my faith
- my moral compass
- my desired outcome
- my ability to effect change in this situation

My faith begged the following questions:

- Why hadn't I prayed for the healing they needed to stop hurting themselves and others?
- Did I really believe they deserved redemption too?
- Did I doubt that God could transform them just as he is transforming me?
- Would I really allow their divisive nature to divide me from my faith, which commands me to pray for those who despitefully use others?

From my moral compass, I asked:

- Was I so stuck in the pain of their actions or the hurt of their words that I failed to see our shared humanity?
- Does their lack of accountability ever make me less accountable for how I show up?

- Would I really allow their actions to compound the hurts of international trauma, national discord, tribalism, and the dark parts of our shared history?

After weeks of contemplating what can be done about other people's actions, their resistance to accountability, and the pretense that ensues, my desire for a healthy outcome and understanding that I can't change others led me to the following important considerations:

- We must release the belief that others should be changed by our expectations. Others are changed by THEIR expectations. While their expectations can include some recognition of our beliefs, they may not; ever.
- We must remember that we are wholly responsible for ourselves—always! We may be tempted to treat others as they are treating others. Unfortunately, their poor behavior does not absolve us of good judgment or good practice. We must respond from this knowledge.
- We must consistently sow what we hope to reap. In response to their unwillingness to take accountability, we may be tempted to manage their behavior or change how we are managing our behavior. Faced with this dilemma, we must consider how we ensure the quality of life we desire. This consideration reminds me that I don't have the time, energy, or responsibility to change others, but I do have the time, energy, and responsibility to manage myself!

There are times when our faith is shaken by the actions of others. It is also true that our moral compass will lead us to a stance that feels divergent from the thinking and practices of others. In these moments, we must ground our actions, emotions, and thoughts in the life we desire for ourselves. We must also temper our approach with the reality of our humanity, not our expectations for other people's capacity.

The Work:

1. Am I consistently sowing the grace, acceptance, and peace I desire to reap?

2. Am I diligently maintaining a posture of openness, care, and unconditional positive regard for others?

3. Am I healing so I may realize my potential, the impact I desire, and partnerships needed to sustain my efforts?

With these new insights or awareness, what commitment will I make to myself or others?

_____

_____

_____

_____

_____

Chapter 100: The Gift of Safe Spaces

We must do more to create safe spaces. It is vital to have spaces where we can let our hair down, take off our masks, and share our truth.

While there should be a safe space within each of us where we are consistently honest with ourselves, it is also important to have a place outside ourselves that allows us to:

- discover we are not alone
- stand in solidarity with others
- grow with support from others
- explore alternative perspectives
- experience intimacy and belonging

I must admit cultivating these spaces can be scary. Fear of judgment can cause us to settle for superficial interactions and counterproductive behaviors like pretending, people pleasing, and hiding. However, it is important to realize that when we choose the safety of superficiality, we lose.

Minimally, we lose the gift of discovering our darkness isn't so great that we can't be loved by others. We also lose the opportunity to establish relationships rooted in authenticity, transparency, and our shared humanity. More troubling, we relegate ourselves to maintaining a mask in our relationships while subtly teaching ourselves we are unworthy of love and support.

This season, I am challenging myself to create and support safe spaces for my family and friends. I am already reaping benefits from doing so. In several recent safe spaces, I received the gift of learning:

- I hadn't failed someone
- That just being present can be enough

- Others have the same fears and challenges
- A strategy for overcoming a long-standing problem

As a result, I am now taking action in some new areas of my life with encouragement from others.

This process has also revealed some critical lessons. Before, when I risked transparency, and it wasn't returned, I felt rejected. I now realize any number of things could have been occurring and I don't have to internalize any of them. Consider this:

- Someone's inability to hear your truth may reflect their discomfort with their own truth.
- No one has to have the same truth, and it's okay if you don't.
- It is possible for many truths to coexist. In fact, they do whether we accept them or not.
- I don't need anyone else's permission to have my truth, but I do need my permission to have self-acceptance.
- Everyone hasn't earned the right to know you and your truth.
- Healthy relationships and people don't weaponize your truth; shame and guilt are unhealthy responses to someone's truth.

It's in safe spaces that we learn these kinds of lessons and unpack our truths. In my new safe spaces, I am finding support, solidarity, and new dimensions of existing relationships.

Not only am I discovering new connections, I am discovering the underpinnings of long-standing connections. I am feeling seen and seeing others with a new level of clarity. The result is a new level of solace, support, and growth.

As I conclude my yearlong reflection journey, I do so with a deeper sense of safety and self.

The Work:

1. How can I foster safe spaces in my networks?

2. What am I doing to ensure my marriage, my home, and other relationships are safe spaces?

3. How can I model for my children, family, and others the practice, power, and value of safe spaces?

With these new insights or awareness, what commitment will I make to myself or others?

_____

_____

_____

_____

_____

Chapter 101: Building on Cracked Foundations

We must attend to the foundation on which we build. If we are to erect our dreams, it must be with consideration for how and where we build.

As you undertake a new effort, are you sure to:

- have proper rest and diet, cognizant that you can only push as far as your physical health will take you
- do it with balance so your effort can be sustained
- do it in partnership with others, recognizing it is impossible to be all things to any project or person

If you answered no to any of these questions, you may be building on a cracked foundation or from the wrong place.

For years, I built or strove incessantly because I was running from poverty. I was wholly consumed by my commitment to providing for my family and being good enough for others.

In time, I discovered that no amount of titles or accolades could make me feel better about myself. Worth is not something we can put on. It must come from within. As my children matured, I also had to develop an identity beyond being a dutiful mom.

Today, I am mindful that the strongest foundation is one founded on running to my dreams instead of running away from my fears.

I am also mindful of the "To-Do List" gone awry. If you maintain a to-do list that routinely does not include the things you need to operate optimally, you may be building on a cracked foundation. Moreover, if you go 48 hours or more without including your needs on your to-do list, you are breaking your foundation.

It is imperative to budget time for rest, renewal, and review. Make time for rest each day. This may feel like a given. However, as a recovering workaholic, I can attest to routinely signing up for overtime and working overtime, while never making time for exercise. When we put this vital task on our to-do list, we are much more likely to accomplish it.

Similarly, we must make time for renewal. It is the only way to effectively renew our efforts. Falsely, we believe we can "pour from empty cups" without consequence. As a heart attack survivor, I can affirm that we all eventually pay the toll for not prioritizing self-care. Now, I make time daily for the renewing of my mind and spirit through prayer, meditation, and grounding.

We must also make time to "review," or check in with ourselves to ensure:

- clarity
- consistency
- connection

I strongly encourage you to check for clarity often. Make it a practice to ask yourself:

- Why am I doing what I do?
- Is this still what I need to be doing?
- Am I leading, living, and loving as I intended?

Also, check for consistency. Ask yourself:

- Is this consistent with values?
- Is it in alignment with my purpose, strengths, and gifts?
- Does it serve my highest good?

Most importantly, ask yourself about maintaining a connection with:

- yourself?
- your support system?

- your purpose?

In the absence of this important inquiry, you may be building on shaky ground!

The Work:

1. How am I ensuring time for the rest, renewal, and review needed?

2. What do I do to maintain a connection?

3. How am I maintaining balance to ensure my efforts are sustainable?

With these new insights or awareness, what commitment will I make to myself or others?

_____

_____

_____

_____

_____

Chapter 102: The Power of Delegation

As a recovering people pleaser, I am embracing the importance of delegation. If you find yourself needing to be everything to everyone, you have an opportunity to evaluate why and reconsider how you are delegating.

Have you ever said or believed:

- only you can do it
- if you don't do it, it won't be done
- no one else can do it like you do it

If you have, it might be time to look inward. More practically, you may not be effectively delegating.

When you are subconsciously trying to perform yourself into worth, you may:

- seek visibility by volunteering for any and everything
- subconsciously adopt a martyr complex
- frequently overextend yourself in your pursuit to demonstrate your value

Moreover, if you are a leader who struggles with setting boundaries, saying no, and/or has low self-esteem, you may be burning out your team, as you volunteer them for everything, have difficulty prioritizing, and routinely seek opportunities for personal visibility.

Even more troubling, you may be robbing your team of opportunities for praise, recognition, or promotion because your esteem has you attention-seeking. As a result, you may even be taking credit for other people's work, ideas, and efforts.

Once you have determined why you are not delegating, consider leveraging delegation as an important tool in the workplace. When used appropriately and effectively, delegation can:

- empower others
- dramatically increase organizational capacity
- reduce burnout
- increase employee engagement
- increase impact and productivity

Beyond these benefits, delegation can also dramatically increase collaboration. As you begin delegating, consider the many opportunities you will have to share impact, resources, and recognition because you delegated! As one step toward leveraging this important professional tool, review your to-do list, project plan, and/or work plan this week and ask:

- Are my strengths being leveraged for their highest best use?
- Am I routinely leveraging the strengths and talents others bring to the organization or issue?
- Have I empowered others to show up in their role, scope, or duties?
- Could the impact be expanded or deepened through collaboration with other internal or external stakeholders, partners, or professionals?
- Have others become increasingly silent or disengaged when I seek to partner with them?
- Am I routinely offering advice or suggestions in areas outside of my professional, personal, or educational experience?
- Am I constantly seeking or accepting responsibilities outside of my area of competency or expertise?

Answering yes to any of these questions consistently may minimally indicate that you have missed an opportunity to delegate.

As you continue your journey, please consider joining me on the journey to effective delegation!

The Work:

1. What am I doing to ensure my strengths, talents, and resources are leveraged for their highest best use?

2. What practices have I put into place to ensure I am leveraging the strengths and talents others bring to the organization or issue?

3. Am I consistently empowering others to show up in their role, scope, duties, and strengths?

With these new insights or awareness, what commitment will I make to myself or others?

_____

_____

_____

_____

_____

Chapter 103: The Relay Race

The relay race is one of the strongest examples of partnership. Each runner is assigned a specific role in completing the race. They must be careful to run their leg without overrunning their role. They must also run in careful coordination with others.

In the absence of fulfilling their role, in coordination with others, the team fails collectively. This requires each runner to be clear about their role and run strongly. It requires the team to communicate consistently and effectively with one another. It requires them to be mindful of transitions. Moreover, they must be mindful that the outcome of any race is a shared result. They either win or lose together.

Similarly, in any organization, department, or team, we must attend to our role, communication, and coordination with others, while being mindful of our shared results and reputation.

As a leader, it is important to distinguish between owning the outcome of the race and being compelled to run every leg.

Early in my leadership journey, I felt compelled to run every leg. Falsely, I believed it was critical to do something in every leg of the race to demonstrate value. Over time, I learned the things I could do to support a successful race were:

- doing my part effectively
- communicating consistently and effectively with the team
- coordinating with others in ways that ensured successful transitions, empowered everyone to run their own leg well, and accounted for what we collectively needed to implement a successful strategy for the race

Moreover, as a leader in a role akin to a coach, I learned I was not running a leg of the race. My role was to support each professional by:

- empowering them to deliver on the potential of their gifts and strengths
- supporting their connection to the mission and vision
- ensuring they understand how their role and strengths contribute to the goal or project at hand
- accounting for and addressing the conditions that impact the work
- providing professionals with the feedback, support, and resources needed to be effective

As I continue my leadership journey, I am finding great value in periodically asking how the relay race is going. Central to this process has been questions like:

- Is everyone clear about the race, including the nature of the field, venue, and participants?
- Is everyone clear about their role in the race? Am I clear about my role in the race?
- Do we have a clear game plan for transitions, obstacles, and opportunities?
- Is everyone engaged? If not, why? How can I increase engagement?
- Is this still the right race or path?

Answering these questions periodically has been invaluable. Whether it's orienting me to ensure everyone is seen, heard, and supported or the ways in which it reinforces introspection, ongoing communication and coordination, and role definition, reviewing how you run your race will take places!

The Work:

1. How am I partnering with others to complete tasks, address issues, and/or ensure success?

2. How am I empowering others to leverage their abilities to meet our shared aims?

3. What can I do to demonstrate trust, affirm capacity, and support productively as I work with others to achieve our shared goals?

With these new insights or awareness, what commitment will I make to myself or others?

_____

_____

_____

_____

_____

Chapter 104: The Unexpected Gift

Today, I encourage you to look for an unexpected gift. It's the gift that may be unwrapped because you were only looking at the loss or heartbreak. It's the thing that may have gone unnoticed in your mourning.

It could be the thing waiting to affirm that all things are working for your good.

Today, as I ponder all of the gifts that have gone unwrapped, I am mindful that it is:

- all of the wrong doors that never opened; even the ones where I was sure it was the job for me, the man for me, or the time for me
- the protection that came dressed as rejection
- the direction that was wrapped in a no, not right now, or a stop
- the ways I was denied the consolation prize because I was destined to win
- the practice I got on the way to my victory

It's everything I thought should be one way that I later discovered was a detour for my safety.

It's how I was pushed out of my comfort zone, pulled into opportunities, and forced to grow.

It's my discomfort zone, my shedding, and the fact that I can learn on a curve.

It's every opportunity that was missed or misunderstood as mine.

So this season, I encourage you to join me in unwrapping the unexpected gifts, the ones we lost sight of when we thought we were losing, but we were just learning.

The Work:

1. How can I embrace the unexpected gifts that result from change, challenge, or tragedy?

2. How can I reframe negative emotions like rejection and find gifts like the direction or protection that sometimes results when we are seemingly denied?

3. What can I learn or gain from what happened unexpectedly? How can I wrap it in ways that give me things like new skills, insights, and opportunities?

With these new insights or awareness, what commitment will I make to myself or others?

_____

_____

_____

_____

_____

Chapter 105: Trust the Process

Recently, I was selected to participate in an executive leadership program as a part of an organization's succession planning efforts. Yesterday's assignment was a focus on crafting personal "rules of leadership." Central to the exercise were three questions:

1. If you are not self-reflective, can you really know yourself?
2. If you don't know yourself, can you really lead yourself?
3. If you can't lead yourself, can you really lead others?

The timing of this exercise was profound. When I began my yearlong commitment to reflection, I had not been selected for this program. I had merely made a commitment to "real resolution" by committing to understanding what was driving my experience, impact, and outcomes. I had eschewed New Year's resolutions or pledges to do the deep work of knowing myself and manifesting my potential.

Hence, to discover that effective leadership is founded on a deep knowing of oneself is so affirming! Many insights have resulted from this journey. Accordingly, when asked to note my evolving "rules of leadership," I noted several principles from my recent reflections, including:

1. People are not our projects. As leaders, our assignment is to foster the conditions requisite for growth.

2. Delegate as an affirmation of your belief in another's capacity, an understanding that sustained change can't be undertaken alone, and with the confidence that you can't and shouldn't be all things to people, projects, or organizations.

3. You have to winnow to win!

4. Always be sure to claim the lesson from the loss.

5. Lean into every transition remembering they are inevitable, constant, and requisite to growth.

As I consider the rich growth resulting from reflection and the gift of this leadership training, I am reminded that things are truly working for my good and that it is okay to trust the process!

The Work:

1. What other evidence affirms that things are working for my good?

2. What tangible examples of my resilience can I leverage when I am feeling unsure, overwhelmed, or disempowered?

3. What is my leadership brand? What am I doing to consistently align my actions with my brand?

With these new insights or awareness, what commitment will I make to myself or others?

_____

_____

_____

_____

_____

Chapter 106: Winnowing to Win

Today, I am mindful of the principle of winnowing. Winnowing is the process of separating wheat from chaff. Just as people who hope to reap a harvest separate the wheat from the chaff, we must separate our worth, wins, and lessons from our pain, shame, and past.

It is only when we separate our identity, gifts, and learning from other people's choices, perceptions, and agendas that we realize our potential.

For many years, I was emotionally entangled in other people's shame, choices, and fears. So much so that their shame became my shame. Even more troubling, I allowed their shame to make me feel ashamed of myself, my upbringing, and conditions.

It is critical for us to root shame out of our lives. If we don't, we fall victim to bias, stereotypes, trauma, and any number of counterproductive experiences. Each of these things can become weights that are crushing!

As a result of separating the emotional wheat and chaff in my life, I am no longer compelled to:

- live down to other people's stereotypes and misconceptions. I can be hurt by them, but I am now able to rebound because I realize that's their issue.
- keep apologizing for myself, others, or someone's unwillingness to change. I'm no longer owning the things and people I cannot change. I'm managing their impact on me by choosing how I think, feel, see, and do.
- accept the labels that have constrained me. I am no one's victim, second choice, mistake, or secret. I am a gift to those who understand and recognize my gifting. First and foremost, I am enough!

As you consider the opportunities to separate the wheat from the chaff, consider these opportunities:

- Have you divorced or ended a relationship? If so, have you taken time to separate the gift of loving from the pain of ending? Have you considered the gifts that resulted along the way, like children or learning more about yourself?
- Have you lost or left a job? If so, have you separated the experience, skill sets, competencies developed, and networking from the ending of the job or tenure?
- Were you raised without a parent or parents? If so, have you separated their physical or emotional absence from the traits, characteristics, gifts, and strengths they did pass on through their DNA? Have you taken the time to notice them so you can use them effectively?
- Have you lost a loved one? If so, have you taken the time to separate their leaving from the gift of their living? Are you actively savoring, honoring, and celebrating the time you did have with them?

Each of these instances is an opportunity to separate the emotional wheat from the chaff.

The Work:

1. What is my opportunity to separate the wheat from the chaff in my leadership? Marriage? Friendships? Family?

2. What am I doing to ensure that insights will be gained and impact made as a result of my ability to discern what is chaff and what is wheat in my life?

3. How will I establish and maintain a practice of winnowing to ensure my growth and success?

With these new insights or awareness, what commitment will I make to myself or others?

_____

_____

_____

_____

_____

Chapter 107: Breadcrumbs

Yesterday, one of my dearest childhood friends called me after reading my magazine publications. She asked me if I remembered a really tough English teacher we had in college and whether I recollected the teacher telling me that I could be an author.

My dear friend also noted how I had always had aspirations. This led me to consider something my husband often notes. He frequently says, "Tiffany, hope and disappointment are always present but you have to choose the one that allows you to move forward!"

Today, as I continue my yearlong commitment to reflection, I am mindful of "breadcrumbs."

Akin to a bird with the potential to fly, I have been led down a path of purpose through "breadcrumbs." Breadcrumbs are a metaphor for the leading of a person to a particular place or path through a subtle signaling of events.

If you have reached this last quarter of the year or this chapter of your life and are asking, "Where am I going?" I encourage you to follow the breadcrumbs.

What may feel like a happenstance occurrence could be a foreshadowing. As I trace the breadcrumbs of my life, I am discovering so many conversations, signals and opportunities to celebrate. Chief among them are:

- Today, my mother reminded me of the time I was caught ditching school. The principal told us that she had reviewed my record and that I owed it to myself and others to do something with my life. She said I had too much potential to let it go to waste.

- My father was murdered while administering a summer youth employment program. Decades later, I would be recruited to administer a federal youth employment program.
- Facing homelessness, I would be recruited to serve as a program coordinator for the McNair Scholars Program, where my assignment was to move into dorms with first-generation college students exploring the prospect of doctoral studies by completing a summer research project. Years later, I would earn a doctorate degree as the first in my family.

Tracing my journey, there are many instances where I have been led purposefully. In each instance, there was the hope of who I could become and the very real disappointment of what was happening at the time. While grief, loss and challenge have been ever present so have reasons to believe, hope and trust—trust that things are working for my good.

As I look back on my journey, I am realizing that nothing has been wasted—no experience, tear, or hurt. Everything that has happened has led to the next place, opportunity, or person. All of it has been leading to who I am becoming.

Accordingly, I ask you to consider where you are being led. What do your triumphs and challenges suggest about your journey or purpose? What are you uniquely positioned to do because of your lived experience, talents, and gifts?

This season, join me in following the breadcrumbs!

The Work:

1. Where am I being led? What do my triumphs and challenges suggest about my journey or purpose? What am I uniquely positioned to do because of my lived experience, talents, and gifts?

2. How can I consistently embrace the purposeful leading underway?

3. How can I be mindful that hope, faith, protection, and provision are also underway when I face a challenge?

With these new insights or awareness, what commitment will I make to myself or others?

_____

_____

_____

_____

_____

Chapter 108: Waiting on Blind Eyes

Today, an exceptional colleague mentioned they were pursuing new aspirations. They lamented feeling invisible and made the bold declarative move of starting a new chapter. Seeing their evident courage, I wrote this reflection about the undervaluing of one's talent: "Waiting on Blind Eyes."

If we're not mindful, we can spend a great deal of time waiting to be seen by others. If you have been waiting for someone to see your talents, realize your contributions, acknowledge your gifts, ask yourself, "Am I in the blind?"

You may be in the inevitable blind spot that results from implicit bias.

You may be too externally focused and blind to your ability to determine your value.

You may be operating in a system that is not designed to see your worth and blind to the ways your professional growth can be supported.

You may be fighting other people's insecurities; individuals who are blind to the ways that high performing teams are a complement of many people's strengths.

You may need to evaluate fit because you have become blinded by golden handcuffs or blind to new possibilities.

In each instance, you have the opportunity to define by whom and how you will be evaluated.

If you don't have a clear sense of your value unless others are consistently affirming it, do the work of knowing who you are no matter the opinion of others.

If you are operating in a system or culture that is not designed to see you, is unable to see you, or unwilling to see you, flip the system or leave the system. Stop waiting on the blinding effect of low aspirations, lowered expectations, and bias to resolve itself.

If your personal and professional relationships leave little room for acknowledgment, leave these toxic relationships and do the work of healing. Empower yourself to identify these toxic dynamics early and choose your peace.

If you are not in a financial position to leave, get strategic! Consider your opportunities to create visibility, foster promotion or co-create change.

One thing is certain, you always have an opportunity to change you. Beyond changing how you see it, how you feel about it and what you do about it, you also have an opportunity to change:

- locations
- positions
- boundaries
- norms
- expectations
- relationships
- stance
- perspective
- strategy

Try changing one or more of these until you find a balance that allows you to maintain:

- dignity
- sense of self-efficacy
- worth
- peace

I am always encouraged by those who take bold steps for their peace. There is also value in smaller strategies and actions, especially if the life you desire requires you to play the long game. So today, join me in getting out of the blind—get a new VISION!

The Work:

1. What am I doing to maintain my sense of self-efficacy and worth in the face of challenge?

2. How can I pivot from seeking external approval and affirmation to ensure that I maintain psychological well-being and sense of worth that is rooted in my expectations, knowledge of myself, and values?

3. What am I doing to define by whom and how I will evaluate my efforts, progress, and impact?

With these new insights or awareness, what commitment will I make to myself or others?

_____

_____

_____

_____

_____

Chapter 109: Have You Prayed for Them

While pondering a recent challenge, I realized I had been praying about some individuals that had harmed others instead of praying for those individuals. This realization led me to this early reflection: Have You Prayed for Them?

Through reflection, I am realizing that I have been praying about troubling people but not praying for the troubled people. This was a painful awareness because it compelled me to ask why.

Why hadn't I prayed for the healing they need to stop hurting themselves and others?

Did I really believe they deserve redemption too?

Did I doubt that God could transform them just as he is transforming me?

Was I so stuck in the pain of their actions or the hurt of their words that I failed to see our shared humanity?

Would I really allow their divisive nature to divide me from my faith, which says pray for those who despitefully use others? Does their lack of accountability ever make me less accountable for how I show up?

Would I really allow their actions to compound the hurts of international trauma, national discord, tribalism and the dark parts of our shared history?

For weeks I have contemplated what is to be done when other people's actions, resistance to accountability and the pretense that ensues feels unmanageable.

If you are contemplating this challenge too, I encourage you to consider these proactive strategies for your own health, healing, and peace:

- Release the belief that others should be changed by your expectations. Others are changed by THEIR expectations. While their expectations can include some recognition of your beliefs, they may not ever.
- Remember that we are wholly responsible for ourselves—always! You may be tempted to treat others as they are treating others. Unfortunately, their poor behavior does not absolve you of good judgment or good practice—act accordingly!
- Consistently sow what you hope to reap. In response to their unwillingness to take accountability, you may be tempted to manage their behavior or change how you are managing your behavior. Faced with this dilemma, I strongly encourage you to consider how you ensure the quality of life you desire. This consideration has reminded me that I don't have the time, energy or responsibility to change others, but I do have the time, energy and responsibility to manage myself!

The Work:

1. How can I be mindful that I am always wholly responsible for myself, while being mindful that I can't be responsible for other people's actions, choices, and perspectives?

2. What actions am I taking to ensure I am always sowing in alignment with my desired results?

3. Am I consistently praying for myself and others? If not, why? How can I make prayer a core life practice?

With these new insights or awareness, what commitment will I make to myself or others?

_____

_____

_____

_____

_____

Chapter 110: I'm Raising Men

"I'm raising a husband and a father!

I had the gift of seeing another boy mom today. I asked how her son was doing and she shared that he had just begun his next chapter, a chapter of independence.

Recognizing that she too had an empty nest, I asked how she was doing and she remarked, "Great! I've been waiting for this moment since his birth. I knew I was raising someone's father and husband. I have given him the skills, morals, and mindset he needs. He is ready!"

This powerful affirmation moved me! As a mother, particularly a mother of sons, I had spent much time raising my sons with a focus on their moral fiber and safety.

Sadly, I had also spent time giving "the talk," almost to the eschewing of topics like what is to be a father or husband. This awareness compelled me to consider the relationship between the role of parenting and Maslow's hierarchy of needs.

I am recognizing that there are instances where we spend so much time just trying to meet our basic needs, things like safety, food, and shelter, that there is little support for actualizing things like being a father and a husband.

Equally troubling is that the fight for survival also leaves little space for fostering belonging.

Raising children alone, working two or three jobs to make ends meet, or starting from a place of trauma or self-esteem invariably encumbers one's ability to aid others in reaching their potential or actualizing.

In this moment, I am mindful of the beauty of knowing someone who knew they were raising someone's husband and father, not only a son.

I am also keenly aware of why we must advocate for things like wage parity, housing access, food security, physical and psychological safety, mental health resources, and the like.

When we do not ensure these resources are available to all, we rob our collective future of the talents and gifts that would have evolved had we ensured that everyone had the conditions to self-actualize.

At this moment, I am also aware of the ways communities living in poverty are disproportionately negatively impacted in actualizing. Before today's discussion, I had not considered in this way how paramount it is to ensure everyone has what they need to reach their potential or this connection to poverty and workforce development.

Workforce development posits that if we arm individuals with the soft and technical skills they need, they can readily respond to economic opportunities and employer needs. It argues that the combination of one's inherent talents and requisite skills are the foundation of social mobility.

This season, I am pondering the impact of people never actualizing those talents because we didn't understand how their basic needs and a sense of belonging are foundational to the skill development that workforce development affords.

We must connect these dots and shore up these areas of the hierarchy if we are to realize the talent that we need for a thriving economy.

The Work:

1. What am I doing to support self-actualization for me and others?

2. How can I work to ensure I am supported to go beyond focusing on my basic needs so I may realize my potential, dreams, and hopes?

3. How can I live a life that inspires my sons and others to commit to their actualization?

With these new insights or awareness, what commitment will I make to myself or others?

_____

_____

_____

_____

_____

Chapter 111: Choosing from a Worth-Based Place

Today, I received news of someone's passing. It compelled me to consider the hidden assumptions that drive my priorities and time.

I think I falsely assume I have time. In this moment, I realize I may not have time. So today I am revisiting everything I have put off, with a commitment to action, alignment and a deeper understanding of choosing from a worth-based place.

When I choose from a worth-based place, I make and maintain time to do the things that serve my wellbeing, peace of mind, soul, heart and health.

When I believe I have worth, I understand that I am an investment.

Like a crop when well tended, I will yield.

Unfortunately, I think we lose sight of the fact that we are like soil. Only what is cultivated will fully yield. Everything else is happenstance.

Even more troubling, there are instances or places in my life where I allow harvest with no stewardship. I hand out my crop to people who won't sow in me, plant or water with me, and in some instances serve as boll weevils in my life.

This season, I'm going to get clear about how interest works. I am either compounding some good things in my life or some bad ones.

When I embrace a worth-based mindset, I understand that I am compounding good health when I eat right and exercise daily. Similarly, when I'm stuffing my emotions and people pleasing myself to exhaustion, I am compounding poor health.

When I choose from a worth-based place, I consistently set and maintain boundaries, empower myself to say no without explanation, and am protective of time—I don't delay or refuse to prioritize my needs while striving to be everyone and everything to others!

Consider what's on your to-do list. Are there things that you have said, you will:

- do someday
- do later—do when time permits
- do when things change
- do when things get better
- do when someone else is ready
- do when the timing is perfect

From a worth-based place, I say to you there is no line on your watch for any of these times. There is also no guarantee they will come.

Have you been waiting to:

- live
- love
- apologize
- put yourself first
- try again
- forgive
- move on
- start

Considering doing them now. From a worth-based place, know that you are deserving of:

- joy
- love
- peace

- health
- happiness

More importantly, recognize that even in bad seasons, on bad days, or in challenging times, that you and the life you desire are worth the fight!

This season and every day forward, I commit to prioritizing and managing my time from a worth-based place.

The Work:

1. What am I doing to determine what I am worthy of and achieve it?

2. What can I do to move from waiting to working on the things I desire?

3. What changes in mindset, practice, or action are needed to have the life I desire?

With these new insights or awareness, what commitment will I make to myself or others?

_____

_____

_____

_____

_____

Chapter 112: Managing the Pendulum, the Clock, and the Scale: The Challenges of Making a Difference

Sometimes, I want to do something, and often it's more than I can do alone.

I am compelled to be the change in the world. Sadly, it feels like the world is changing faster than I can make a difference, but too slow for me to see the difference in my lifetime.

I'm left with the dilemma of figuring out what I can do, with the time I have, in shifting winds, with a penchant for justice.

As I unpack this challenge, I am mindful of the pendulum, clock, and scale.

An inherent part of my work is managing the ways in which social issues become politicized. I liken it to a pendulum swinging to and fro. One minute, my thinking, position, and wording are timely, and in another moment, I am canceled.

It's not just that the issue has become unpopular, it's the likelihood of being silenced again, invisible and forgotten that has me troubled.

I think my work here is to see these swings as seasons, be fully who I am, do what I can, and be okay if the moment has passed.

I'm also managing a clock. The older I get, the more I realize I have a finite amount of time. More troubling, my mistakes and regrets feel like wasted time. Each regret seemingly shortens my clock, almost like an egg timer whose seal is seeping.

I worry that if I had come into my voice or purpose sooner, I could be doing more.

It also feels like an errant clock armed with an alarm that begins sounding as the time ticks down or like a bad episode of Jeopardy where I'm doubling down on the wrong answers.

I think my work here is to trust God's timing and harken to Angelou's declaration, "When I knew better, I did better."

I am also managing a scale in a world where I've been told the arc bends toward justice.

Some days, I don't feel like I can see the arc at all. I worry things are so off balance that my dreams and hopes will be crushed under the weight of insecurity and tribalism.

I'm still sorting out my work in this area. I think I can strive to remain hopeful, at least minimally.

As I consider the totality of managing the pendulum, clock, and scale, I think I have an opportunity to:

- See the swings of the pendulum as seasons, recognizing that life can be cyclical, that we often repeat history, and that progress is incremental—there will probably be another season to try again.
- Consider that the ticking of the clock is me "should-ing" on myself again, giving the reins to my perfectionism and fear of failure again, and forgetting to be at peace with my best effort and progress.
- Remember that I have greater influence over the scale of maintaining my own balance; I can actively work to ensure I'm maintaining a work-life balance, having a balance of perspectives, and leveraging a balance of strategies.

This season, I will commit to not being driven by the pendulum, clock, or scale but mindful of the ways in which each of these constructs represents my unconscious expectations, whether reasonable or unreasonable.

So, my work will be striving to maintain and operate from reasonable expectations.

The Work:

1. How can I define the challenges I face in ways that allow for actionable, attainable, sustainable solutions?

2. How can I consistently incorporate grace, patience, support, and rest into my approach?

3. Where are the clocks, scales, and pendulums currently showing up in my life? Have I acknowledged them and unpacked them? What hidden or explicit beliefs are perpetuating them? How do I reframe them to establish and maintain a healthy balance?

With these new insights or awareness, what commitment will I make to myself or others?

_____

_____

_____

_____

_____

Chapter 113: Don't Be Afraid to Repot Yourself!

This yearlong reflection journey has brought much awareness. Recently, an incredible leader in my life shared a profound analogy about "repotting." Here's my reflection from our discussion.

If we are to realize our potential, we must be willing to repot ourselves. We must allow for:

- the recognition that we have grown beyond where we are
- the space needed to continue our growth
- change; a change in perspective, place, or relationships—most importantly, ourselves

It is also important to note that recognition that we need more isn't or does not have to be an eschewing of our humble beginnings, past relationships, or the decisions that got us to where we are. Rather, we can be grateful for our journey and allow ourselves to prepare for and expect more.

Like the proverbial plant, if we allow ourselves to continue to grow, we should anticipate that we will reach a place in our lives where our capacity, aptitude, or the conditions demand that we create space for our flowering. It's from a place that we should ask ourselves:

- Where in my life have I grown to the edges of my mindset, relationships, or situation?
- Where might I realize more of who I am, my purpose, or impact if I accepted I have grown beyond what can be realized in this place, space, or time?
- Where or for whom might my gifts, thinking, or talents be a viable solution if I accepted that I have done what I can here?

Our unwillingness to ask these questions will only lead to a poor fit, stagnation, apathy, or strife. Accordingly, we must have the courage to ask ourselves if it is time for repotting.

This season, I encourage you to be open to growth!

The Work:

1. In what areas of my life have I grown beyond the utility of my practices?

2. Have I outgrown the relationships where I spend most of my time, seek advice, or seek approval?

3. What new opportunities lie ahead if I find the courage to start something new, try again, or be open to change?

With these new insights or awareness, what commitment will I make to myself or others?

_____

_____

_____

_____

_____

Chapter 114: And If This Is the Last Day

Over the course of my yearlong reflection journey, I realized that I had been waiting. I was waiting to live. I was telling myself some false things about time. I said things like:

- "I will have time later.'
- "I don't have time now."
- "The time is not right."
- "The time is now or never."
- "In time, it will happen."
- "Time heals all wounds."
- "Time is of the essence."
- "There's no time like the present."

After much reflection, I realize that some, all, or none of these "time truths" have felt true at different crossroads in my life. While reflecting on why I am waiting, I wrote "And If Today Is the Last Day." I hope you will consider if you have been waiting. Moreover, I pray, you have not been holding your breath, fears, or hurts while waiting to live a life that is waiting on you. Here's my reflection from waiting to live the life that I want:

If you knew today was the last day, would you allow yourself to be ruled by fear? Would you still hold onto the grudge? Would you still struggle to apologize or struggle with the apology you never received?

Of all the things you are holding, would you still hold onto shame, fear, or grief?

If this was the last day, would you be the last to:

- call
- say, "I'm sorry"

- forgive

Would you move from dreaming and wishing to action?

Would you spend the last day living?

Would you finally say what you have been thinking?

Would you finally do what you have been hoping?

Would you finally:

- be honest?
- be happy?
- be satisfied?
- BE?

If the answer is yes to any of these questions, let today be the last day!

Let today be the last day you settle for living a life below your dreams!

Often, we believe that we have time. We believe that we have the luxury of holding out, holding on, and holding in. We hold out for others to apologize first. We hold on to our hurts no matter how toxic. We hold in how we really feel, our expectations and desires.

We wait for the clock to strike "perfect" as if there is some precise time for us to be happy or start.

We tell ourselves someone else has to go first, as we live as though it's not okay to put ourselves first.

We hunger for acceptance, but we won't give it to ourselves. We hope others will finally realize:

- what we need from them
- what we think
- how we feel

We do this while neglecting to realize that it is nearly impossible to meet an unstated need, desire, or hope.

So this season, I encourage you to live like it's your last day. I want you to:

- forgive everyone you need to forgive
- apologize to everyone who believes you owe them an apology; it will cost you nothing
- decide to be happy
- accept yourself without exception
- love without restraint
- experience joy
- laugh heartily
- dwell in peace
- have gratitude
- be excited

Let's make today the last day we do otherwise!

If you have been waiting to live, consider this exercise. Consider your ideal life. List how your life looks, sounds and feels in each of the major domains of your life. Some key areas to note are how would you be living:

- spiritually
- professionally
- in relationships
- healthwise
- in leisure
- in purpose

As you give vision to each of the areas, be sure to list them in actionable ways. Go beyond writing a statement like "I would have a great relationship with my family." Think about what it would mean to have a great relationship in ways that you can consistently see, hear, and feel that the relationship is great.

As a next step, note it in ways that it can become a roadmap or framework for achieving your desired life. Be sure to note the quality and specific behavior that will occur in your great relationship. Go from waiting for it to happen to defining it, its steps, and a plan for achieving it.

The Work:

1. How will I demonstrate my commitment to living fully?

2. In what areas of my life will I commit to living more fully immediately? How will it look, sound, and feel when I am living fully in these areas? How will I hold myself accountable to fully living in these areas?

3. Who do I need to forgive now? To whom do I need to apologize now? Where do I need to be truthful with myself or others? What do I need to release now? What do I need to embrace to have the life I desire?

With these new insights or awareness, what commitment will I make to myself or others?

_____

_____

_____

_____

_____

As I consider the insights and awareness gleaned from this season, what commitments to myself or others am I measuring, monitoring, and adjusting as needed, to ensure my success?

_____

_____

_____

_____

_____

_____

_____

_____

_____

_____

_____

_____

_____

_____

_____

_____

Get Your Copy Today!
#TheJourneyInward
The Journey Inward: Four Seasons of Reflection for Deep Healing and Transformation

By Tiffany Tyler-Garner, PhD

The Journey Inward: Four Seasons of Reflection for Deep Healing and Transformation is the personal development book of its day! It chronicles a year long journey of exploration designed to help readers unearth limiting beliefs so they may realize the life of their dreams. Written by Dr. Tiffany Tyler-Garner, a psychologist, published researcher, and proven servant leader, the book provides practical strategies for overcoming imposter syndrome, trauma, and codependence, while affording readers the psychological safety of empathy, compassion, and solidarity.

Ready to Grow?

If you're ready to embark on a transformative journey, whether it's growing your organization, healing from trauma, or tackling complex social issues through programming, I invite you to connect with me. Let's start a conversation about how my consulting services in nonprofit and business development, grant writing, program development, evaluation, and technical assistance can support your goals. Together, we can write a powerful new chapter of growth and healing. For more information, visit www.drtylerinspires.com.

About the Author

Dr. Tiffany Tyler-Garner is an educational psychologist, published researcher, and thought leader. Her personal and professional achievements reveal a servant leader committed to transforming the conditions that impact children, families and communities. Currently, Dr. Tyler-Garner spearheads workforce development and social initiatives for the City of Las Vegas.

Prior to joining the City, Dr. Tyler-Garner served as the executive director of the Children's Advocacy Alliance, a 23+ year child policy advocacy organization. Dr. Tyler-Garner's professional journey also includes serving as a gubernatorial cabinet member, CEO of an affiliate of the nation's largest dropout prevention organization, Communities in Schools, and the COO of a White House-recognized workforce development nonprofit organization, Nevada Partners, Incorporated.

In each of these roles, Dr. Tyler-Garner has been a champion for opportunity while spearheading the delivery of programs, policy and services to improve conditions for Nevada's most vulnerable populations. Moreover, Dr. Tyler-Garner has a rich history of service that includes serving on an array of governmental and nonprofit boards and commissions, including the Nevada Children's Commission, Clark County Juvenile Justice Services Citizen Advisory Committee, the Las Vegas Metropolitan Police Department's Multicultural Advisory Council, the Nevada Sentencing Commission, the Nevada Governor's Office of Economic Development Board, the Nevada Governor's Office of Workforce Development Board, the Nevada Patient Protection Commission, Communities in Schools of Nevada, Hope for Prisoners, Obodo Collective, and Women of Global Change.

Dr. Tyler-Garner is also a member of Alpha Kappa Alpha, Incorporated, the nation's first intercollegiate historically African American sorority, where she serves as chaplain for her local chapter. She is also a member of the National Coalition of 100 Black Women where she works to improve conditions for women and girls in areas of health, education and economic empowerment. Committed to an unwavering investment in social change, Dr. Tyler-Garner is also a member of The Links, Incorporated, an elite international women's service organization whose focus is community service, advocacy and education.

Dr. Tyler-Garner's commendations include the Urban Chamber of Commerce's Women Business Advocate award, Vegas Inc.'s Humanitarian of the Year award, Workforce Connections' Workforce Development Champion of the Year award, and UNLV College of Education Alumna of the Year award. Dr. Tyler holds a Doctorate in Educational Psychology for the University of Nevada- Las Vegas, a Master of Science in Counseling from California State University-Northridge, and Bachelor of Arts in Psychology and Sociology from the University of Southern California.

When Dr. Tyler-Garner is not leading or serving, you can find her empowering professionals businesses, and communities in the areas of personal development, professional development, program development, program evaluation, grants management and grant writing. To learn more about Dr. Tyler-Garner and how she empower you, visit www.drtylerinspires.com.